Moira Butterfield

Hi... we're Amelia and Marco and we've created 19 awesome trails for you to follow.

The pushpins on this map mark the starting points, and each trail is guaranteed to let you in on some of the city's secrets and blow your mind with loads of cool facts. So whether you are a foodie, a sports fanatic, or a movie expert, this book has got something for you!

CONTENTS

PAGE NUMBER

SPECIAL STREETS

To qualify for a cabbie's badge, London cab drivers have to learn the names of over 60,000 roads in central London. Not surprisingly, it takes them years, but you can take a shortcut and discover some of the capital city's most interesting streets right here.

ST. MARTIN-IN-THE-FIELDS CHURCH PATH WC2

CITY OF WESTMINSTER

THE LONGEST STREET NAME IN LONDON IS IN THE BOROUGH OF WESTMINSTER.

ABBEY ROAD

DOOR OF POWER

10 DOWNING STREET

Britain's prime minister (PM) lives at Number 10 Downing Street. Here, for nearly three centuries, PMs have eaten, drunk, snoozed, and run the country (not necessarily all at the same time!). PMs are never given the keys to their home, though. Armed guards have to let them in and out.

NUMBER 10 IS ONE OF THE MOST HEAVILY GUARDED BUILDINGS IN BRITAIN, AND IT'S EVEN PROTECTED FROM MICE. IT HAS ITS OWN CAT, WITH THE OFFICIAL TITLE CHIEF MOUSER.

SNAP STREET

ABBEY ROAD PEDESTRIAN CROSSING

Cameras at the ready, everyone! Visitors from across the globe stride across the Abbey Road pedestrian crossing all day long, while their friends take photos – and all because of a world-famous supergroup.

A PIECE OF THE PAST

LITTLE COMPTON STREET

London is thousands of years old, and there is a lot of past life buried under its streets. Who knows what long-gone secrets lurk deep beneath the feet of today's Londoners? A little glimpse of the past can be seen hidden below a street grating in the Soho area of London. Here lies Little Compton Street, an old lane where Londoners once walked. New buildings were built over it in 1896, but it remains in the shadows along with its street sign.

LITTLE COMPTON STREET

CARTING LANE

The Beatles posed here for the cover of their *Abbey Road* album, released in 1969. It sold millions, and music fans have been re-creating the cover shot ever since.

Check out the webcam online – the Abbey Road Crossing Cam – and watch people holding up traffic on Abbey Road in real time. Then search for the album cover itself and spot American tourist Paul Cole. He was photographed standing in the background of the iconic cover shot and became accidentally famous.

STINKY SWITCH-ON

CARTING LANE

Walk this way for smelliness. Carting Lane was once nicknamed Farting Lane because, until the 1950s, its street lamps were powered partly by waste gas from London's sewage. Locals used to joke that guests at the nearby super-posh Savoy Hotel caused the lamps to flicker when they broke wind. These days the lamps are powered by gas from the gas main, but the nickname has hung around like a bad smell.

SIDEWAYS SHUFFLE

EMERALD COURT

Emerald Court is London's narrowest street. It's a teeny-weeny walled alleyway, and most people have to shuffle through sideways, since it only measures a shoulder-squeezing 26 inches (66 cm) wide. Now take a guess at London's shortest street name. You may never find it... It's a road called Hide!

EMERALD COURT

THE DEVIL DID IT

BLEEDING HEART YARD

Bleeding Heart Yard is the location of one of London's most ghoulish legends. The story goes that a woman called Lady Elizabeth Hatton made a pact with the devil to get wealth, power, and a mansion. At her housewarming party in 1626, she made the fatal mistake of dancing with the devil himself, who spirited her off. All that was found the next day was a bleeding heart lying on the road outside. Ouch!

According to historians, the Hatton story is definitely not true, but nobody takes any notice of those killjoys, and the horrible heart tale still gets told. Try telling it yourself, preferably on a dark and spooky night...

WONDER WALLS

REDCHURCH STREET

Shoreditch is an area of London where street art is especially popular. Top of the paint-tastic wonder-wall list is Redchurch Street. It's a rainbow of street art, with monsters, cyber goblins, and neon letters dazzling passers-by in between the shops and restaurants.

search: CHEWING GUM

6.7 TONS

Around 6.7 tons of chewing gum gets dropped in London's West End every year.

15.5 MILLION

It costs around US$15.5 million a year to clean the chewing gum off London's sidewalks. That's an average of US$1.90 per piece.

ONE OF THE WORLD'S MOST FAMOUS STREET ARTISTS, BANKSY, LIKES TO LEAVE HIS MARK IN THIS AREA OF LONDON, AND HIS WORK HAS BEEN KNOWN TO POP UP OVERNIGHT. HE'S CAREFUL THAT NO ONE SPOTS HIM WHILE HE MAKES HIS MASTERPIECES, AND NOBODY KNOWS WHAT HE LOOKS LIKE!

LONDON BY JET PACK

Let's put on some rocket-powered jet packs – the kind that can take us soaring over London's rooftops. Then we can go hunting for wondrous sights high up above everybody else. Are you ready? OK. Let's GO!

LONDON EYE

443 FT. (135 M) TALL
394 FT. (120 M) WIDE

ROOFTOP ROOTS

THE ROOF GARDENS, KENSINGTON

There are dozens of secret green spaces above London, some belonging to office buildings and apartments, others open to anyone. The Roof Gardens in Kensington is the biggest example. It's an oasis perched on top of a department store, with fountains, arches, a fish-filled stream, lots of trees, and even a flock of flamingos preening in its ponds. The flamingos don't seem to mind living on the roof of a store, and their home is a lush hideaway for stressed city folk.

100 FT. HIGH

WHEELY GOOD VIEW

LONDON EYE

The London Eye is the world's biggest rotating cantilevered observation wheel ("cantilevered" means it's supported at one end). It offers a great view, up to 25 miles (40 km) away on a clear day (that's about as far as Windsor Castle, so remember to wave to the queen!). It can carry 800 people at a time, and more than 3.5 million people cram into its 32 passenger compartments every year. That's more people than visit the Egyptian pyramids or India's Taj Mahal.

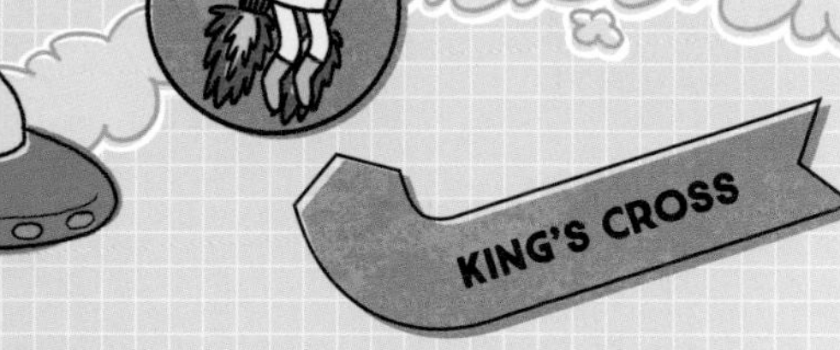

68 FT. (21 M) HIGH

CLEO'S COLUMN (NOT)

CLEOPATRA'S NEEDLE

A little piece of Egypt, called Cleopatra's Needle, sits on Victoria Embankment. It's around 3,460 years old and comes from an ancient city called Heliopolis. The hieroglyphs carved all over it commemorate Ancient Egyptian battle victories, and are actually nothing to do with Cleopatra. It was given to Britain in the 1800s by the ruler of Egypt, and shipped by boat to the UK. During the voyage, a storm killed six crewmen, and the needle was nearly lost for good, leading people to say it was cursed. When it finally arrived, it was given its nickname by locals. Pharaoh 'nuff!

THE VICTORIANS BURIED A TIME CAPSULE UNDER THE NEEDLE. AMONG OTHER THINGS, IT IS SAID TO CONTAIN TOYS, A BABY BOTTLE, A TRAIN TIMETABLE, AND PICTURES OF BEAUTIFUL VICTORIAN WOMEN.

DID THE ALIENS LAND?

KING'S CROSS STATION

Some London buildings have a roof that gives them a wow factor, and King's Cross Station is a good example. A vast white fan-shaped roof stretches across it, and modern metal ribs ripple out from its Victorian red-brick walls, almost as if a spaceship has landed. Tens of millions of passengers a year visit the station and get to look up at its beautiful hi-tech ceiling.

ST. BRIDE'S CHURCH

OXO TOWER

THE MONUMENT

SNEAKY SPELLING

OXO TOWER

When this lofty spot on London's South Bank was bought by a company that made OXO stock cubes, they wanted to put their name up in lights. Banned from putting up a flashy advertisement, they had a clever backup plan. They built the windows of the tower in shapes that just so happened to resemble an O, an X, and another O. Everybody still calls it the OXO Tower, even though the original cunning company has left and it's now full of shops and restaurants.

UP IN FLAMES

THE MONUMENT

In 1666, the Great Fire of London started in a bakery in Pudding Lane and soon swept through the whole city, destroying thousands of homes. The fire is commemorated by the Monument – the world's tallest individual stone column. Its height is the exact distance from the column to the place where the fire began, and the gleaming golden urn on top symbolizes flames. Anyone who climbs the 311 stairs gets a certificate for reaching the top.

WEDDING WONDER

ST. BRIDE'S CHURCH

Churches have graced this spot for thousands of years, but today's church was built after the Great Fire of London, when famed architect Sir Christopher Wren agreed to give the ruined building a majestic makeover. The steeple has five white sections one on top of the other, and it's said to have inspired the design of wedding cakes.

ST. BRIDE'S CHURCH
226 FT. (69 M)

OXO TOWER
175 FT. (53.3 M)

THE MONUMENT
200 FT. (61 M)

LEADENHALL BUILDING
735 FT. (224 M)

30 ST. MARY AXE
591 FT. (180 M)

20 FENCHURCH STREET
525 FT. (160 M)

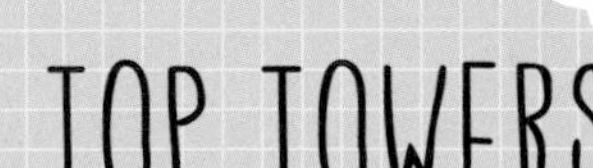

TOP TOWERS

THE CHEESEGRATER, GHERKIN, AND WALKIE-TALKIE

Locals have a habit of giving London skyscrapers nicknames. There's the Cheesegrater (actually the Leadenhall Building), London's second-tallest building, which has an angled edge. There's the Gherkin (30 St. Mary Axe), which is cucumber-shaped with enough glass panels to cover three soccer fields. Then there's the Walkie-Talkie (20 Fenchurch Street). It got renamed the Walkie Scorchie or the Fryscraper when light reflecting off its mirrored surface caused beams hot enough to melt holes in cars on the street below. The architects had to cover the surface with nonreflective film to stop the destructive rays!

LONDON'S HIGHEST GARDEN, THE SKY GARDEN, GROWS UNDER A GIANT GLASS DOME ON TOP OF THE WALKIE-TALKIE BUILDING.

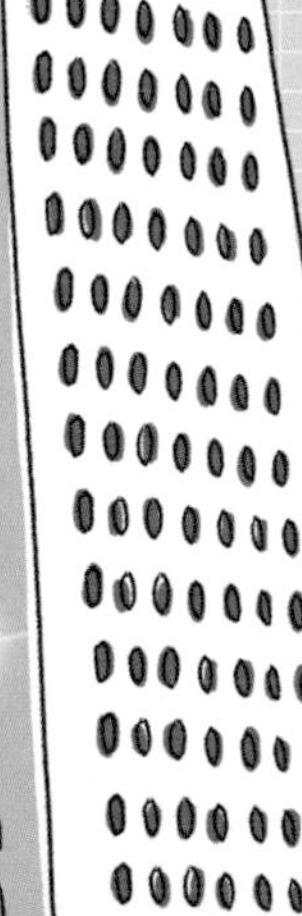

HIGHEST IN TOWN

THE SHARD

The Shard is the highest skyscraper in Europe, and gives the highest view of London, from a viewing platform 800 feet (244 m) up. The architect decided he wanted the building to look as if it was rising like an iceberg from the river nearby.

THE SHARD

1,015.7 FT. (309.6 M) HIGH

SHARD SHIVERS

The crane operators who helped build the Shard worked nearly 1,000 feet (310 m) high and could feel the vibrations from jet aircraft flying above them.

1,015.7 FT. (309.6 M) HIGH

72 FLOORS

306 FLIGHTS OF STAIRS

US$759 MILLION

The soaring skyscraper cost upwards of US$759 million. At one point, 7,000 cubic yards (5,400 cubic meters) of concrete were being poured every three minutes.

CRAZY CLIMBING

The Shard has attracted some unlikely adventurers, with climbers, abseilers, and even parachutists using it as the ultimate urban challenge.

FEARLESS FOX

When the Shard was being built, a fox managed to get in and climbed up to the 72nd floor, where he survived for a couple of weeks by eating food scraps left lying around by the builders. When he was discovered, staff nicknamed him Romeo. He was rescued, checked by a vet, and then set free, back to his roaming life on the streets of London.

BRAVEST JOB IN TOWN!

THE SHARD'S WINDOW CLEANERS ABSEIL DOWN THE BUILDING, POLISHING 11,000 GLASS PANELS (AN AREA EQUIVALENT TO EIGHT SOCCER FIELDS). IT TAKES A WEEK TO CLEAN JUST ONE SIDE OF THE BUILDING. THEY WORK FROM PLATFORMS CALLED WINDOW-CLEANING BASKETS, BUT IN 2012, ONE WINDOW CLEANER HAD TO BE RESCUED WHEN HE GOT TRAPPED IN A BASKET THAT BEGAN TO SWING IN HIGH WINDS.

search: **FUTURE SKYLINE**

A CAN OF HAM?

Lots of new skyscrapers are planned for London's skyline, including some unusual shapes that are bound to get interesting nicknames when they are finished. Current plans include buildings that look like a can of ham, a giant sail, and a giant rolled-up newspaper.

TUNNEL UNDER LONDON

There's a whole world of tunnels, underground rivers, and secret spaces under London. Let's turn on our flashlights, crawl down there, and take a look!

DEEPLY TASTY

98 FT. (30 M) UNDERGROUND

CLAPHAM NORTH DEEP AIR-RAID SHELTERS

A group of old World War II air-raid shelters, hidden deep under Clapham, are being reused in interesting new ways. Documents and film archives are stored down there, and one area has even become an underground farm. LED lights plus water gathered from underground help shelves of mini-vegetables, herbs, and salad crops to grow all year round, ready for use in London restaurants.

LONDON LABYRINTHS

CAMDEN & CLERKENWELL CATACOMBS

Beneath the busy streets of Camden Town there is a labyrinth of abandoned catacombs (tunnels), which were used as horse stables and underground warehouses 200 years ago. The risk of flooding (and general spookiness) means they're off-limits to visitors. Further to the east, a set of tunnels called the Clerkenwell Catacombs has a horrible history as a prison, The House of Detention, dating back to 1617.

NOT SURPRISINGLY, CLERKENWELL'S PRISON CAVERNS ARE SAID TO BE HAUNTED. VISITORS HAVE REPORTED SHADOWY FIGURES STALKING THEM, PLUS GHOSTLY SOBBING. EEK! LET'S MOVE ON QUICKLY!

CLAPHAM NORTH

CAMDEN TOWN

THE LONDON UNDERGROUND TUBE SYSTEM

250 MILES

The Underground System covers about 250 miles (402 km) around London.

About 45 percent of it is actually in tunnels.

190 FT. (58 M)

Hampstead (left) is the deepest station, at 190 feet (58 m).

1.03 BILLION

Around 1.03 billion passengers travel on the Tube every year.

UNDERGROUND GHOSTS

ALDWYCH UNDERGROUND STATION

Over 40 Underground stations are "ghost stations." That doesn't mean they're special stops for spooks. It means they're left empty and unused. One of these ghost stations, Aldwych, is kept as a museum piece and is often used as a set by film and TV companies.

TOP-SECRET SPOT

CABINET WAR ROOMS

Winston Churchill led Britain through World War II in a top-secret subterranean hideout right in the middle of London. This underground control center would once have been buzzing with military types poring over maps and having vital meetings as German planes rained bombs down above. It was shut in 1945, at the end of the war, and not reopened until 1975, when the world learned about it for the very first time. The rooms are kept as they were left, with wartime maps scattered around and lifelike models of people carrying out their jobs.

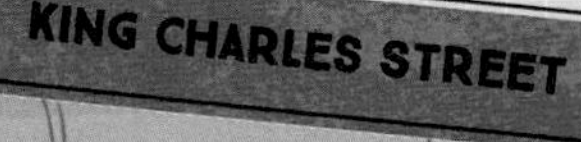

ALDWYCH STATION

Drown'd puppies, stinking sprats, all drench'd in mud, dead cats, and turnip-tops, come tumbling down the flood.

Author Jonathan Swift wrote a poem (above) in 1710 describing the festering Fleet after a rain shower.

SECRET RIVERS

THE RIVER FLEET

London has lots of hidden river tributaries flowing beneath its streets towards the Thames. Gradually they've been built over, until most of them now flow entirely underground. The biggest is the River Fleet, and you can spot its mouth under Blackfriars Bridge. Centuries ago it was a major city river, but it was badly polluted.

BOOKS BELOW

BRITISH LIBRARY

London's British Library has around 150 million items, so it's not surprising that it needs plenty of space. Beneath the library building there are four big underground levels, mostly filled with shelves of books, in a temperature-controlled environment that helps preserve paper. Some of the most valuable books and manuscripts are in special chambers filled with inergen, a harmless mixture of gases that helps to prevent fire from breaking out.

A GIANT ELECTRONIC CONVEYOR BELT SNAKES AROUND THE BRITISH LIBRARY, BRINGING UP BOOKS FROM BELOW.

BLACKFRIARS BRIDGE

BRITISH LIBRARY

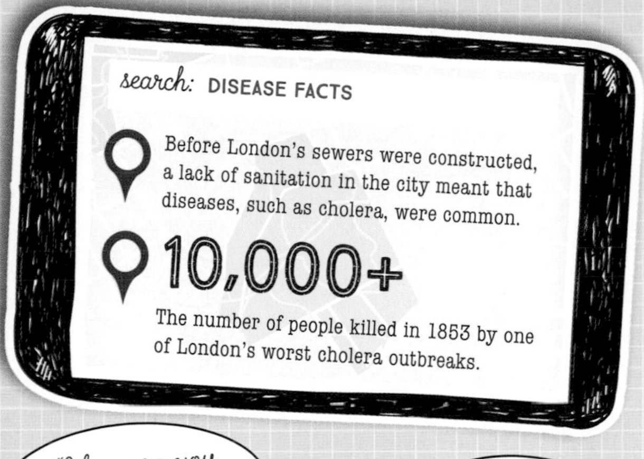

SMELLS AND STINKS

LONDON SEWERS

London's sewage was once dumped into the River Thames, leading to sickening smells and deadly diseases swirling around town. Enter Joseph Bazalgette, who built 82 miles (132 km) of brick-lined underground sewers to carry the waste, linked by pumping stations to keep the flow going. His sewers still wend their way beneath London today. Sewage cleaners work to keep the tunnels clean, removing lots of "fatbergs" – giant lumps of congealed cooking oil that regularly block the tunnels. One "fatberg" discovered under Leicester Square was big enough to fill nine double-decker buses!

RIVER OF SKULLS

THE WALBROOK

The Walbrook is another of London's hidden underground streams, running close to the Bank of England under the City of London. In Roman times it flowed aboveground, and during modern building construction, lots of ancient human skulls have been discovered on the riverbed. It's possible that some of them were thrown in by local people to please river gods, or perhaps they washed into the river from burial sites. Some of the skulls show violent injuries, and might even be the heads of Roman gladiators.

THE WALBROOK

LEICESTER SQUARE

TREASURE HUNT

Legend has it that a young man called Dick Whittington came to London to seek his fortune because he'd heard the streets were paved with gold. The sidewalks might not be made of gold exactly, but it's true that London is awash with cash! Follow the golden pathway to find the capital's most glittering and expensive treasure spots.

THE LEGEND GOES THAT DICK WHITTINGTON EVENTUALLY BECAME ONE OF LONDON'S SUPER-RICH, AND BECAME LORD MAYOR!

ROYAL MEWS BUCKINGHAM PALACE

VICTORIA AND ALBERT MUSEUM

BLING BEASTIES

GLOUCESTER CANDLESTICK

The Victoria and Albert Museum is home to thousands of gorgeous glittery treasures from the past, including the Gloucester Candlestick, made for a church around 1,000 years ago. Dragons, monkeys, and other busy beasties climb up the candlestick, biting each other or whispering to each other as they grab onto flowers and plants.

SHINY RIDE

GOLD STATE CARRIAGE

The Gold State Carriage carries British monarchs through London streets on special occasions. It's made of gold-painted wood, and it's so heavy it needs eight horses to pull it. It's around 200 years old, and riding inside it is apparently so bumpy that it feels like being on a boat in rough seas. Queen Victoria found it so wobbly that she refused to use it.

TOP HOME ON THE PLANET

BUCKINGHAM PALACE

The London home of the British monarch is officially the world's most expensive home, worth over US$1.5 billion. Its most dazzling room, the Throne Room, has walls bedecked in scarlet and gold, and velvet chairs with golden sphinx-shaped armrests. However, when Prince William had his wedding reception in Buckingham Palace, it was turned into a "chillax" room with its own DJ.

BURIED GOLD

FISHPOOL HOARD

Around 460 years ago, someone was on the run and had to bury a fortune fast! That's thought to be the story behind the Fishpool Hoard – 1,237 gold coins plus jewelry – now on display at the British Museum. It was a time of rebellion in Britain, and the person who buried the stash could have been on the losing side of a battle.

THE FISHPOOL HOARD WAS WORTH A GREAT DEAL WHEN IT WAS BURIED – AROUND US$459,570 IN TODAY'S MONEY.

GEM CENTRAL

HATTON GARDEN

This area is London's jewelry district, where gems are bought and sold and fine jewelry is created. Early in 2015, a gang of robbers drilled through 20 inches (50.8 cm) of concrete into a Hatton Garden bank vault and stole gems worth up to US$310 million. It was one of the biggest robberies ever in Britain, but eventually the gang was caught.

SILVERY STORE

SILVER VAULTS

LONDON SILVER VAULTS

This underground labyrinth was once for wealthy Londoners to store their valuables. The vaults were protected by guards with cudgels, cutlasses, and shotguns, and you can still see the thick iron-lined doors that stopped thieves from making away with treasures. Now it is the glittery home of London's top silver shops.

search: TREASURE FACTS

US$2.6 TRILLION

The official value of all of London's homes put together.

BRITAIN'S RICHEST ROAD

Bishop's Avenue, Highgate

This road has been given the nickname "Billionaire's Row" for being the most expensive street of homes in Britain.

Mansions here sell for up to US$100 million.

PRICIEST UK PARKING

Near Albert Hall

Paying for parking in London can mean handing over a fortune! In 2014, a two-car parking space near the Albert Hall was sold for US$616,692.

PROTECTED GOLDEN PILE

BANK OF ENGLAND

Gold bars worth around US$239 billion are stored in an underground vault under the Bank of England, behind bombproof walls. The gold belongs to governments around the world. It's a bank worker's job to regularly dust the bars.

MANSION HOUSE

BANK OF ENGLAND

LORD MAYOR'S STASH

MANSION HOUSE TREASURES

The Mansion House is the home of the lord mayor of the City of London, and it's where the lord mayor's treasures are kept. These include the State Sword and the Mace, shown above, and a Chain of Office made of gold and diamonds. One of the biggest gold and silver plate collections in the world is kept here for grand banquets. A centuries-old sword, the Pearl Sword, is here, too. It has a scabbard sewn with 2,500 pearls and it was once used by Queen Elizabeth I in ceremonies.

BRITAIN'S BILLIONS

THE CROWN JEWELS

TOWER OF LONDON

The British Crown Jewels include ten, yes ten, crowns! There are also swords, orbs, scepters, and other bling things needed to crown British monarchs. The whole super-shiny collection is kept behind extra-thick toughened glass and protected by the latest hi-tech security in the Jewel House of the Tower of London. That's because it's worth...

... US$5–8 billion!

GEMTASTIC!

The Imperial State Crown, shown here, has several special gems that are so big they get their own names. The oldest one is probably St. Edward's Sapphire (the blue stone in the middle of the cross on top). It's said to be from a ring worn by Edward the Confessor, king of England nearly 1,000 years ago, and it has a spooky past. Edward's grave was opened and it was taken from his finger some years after he died.

HOLD THIS, YOUR MAJESTY

A golden orb and a jewel-encrusted scepter are handed to the monarch at the crowning ceremony, along with a sword and some gold armlets. At the same time, the monarch is dabbed on the head, hands, and chest with holy oil from a sacred silver spoon.

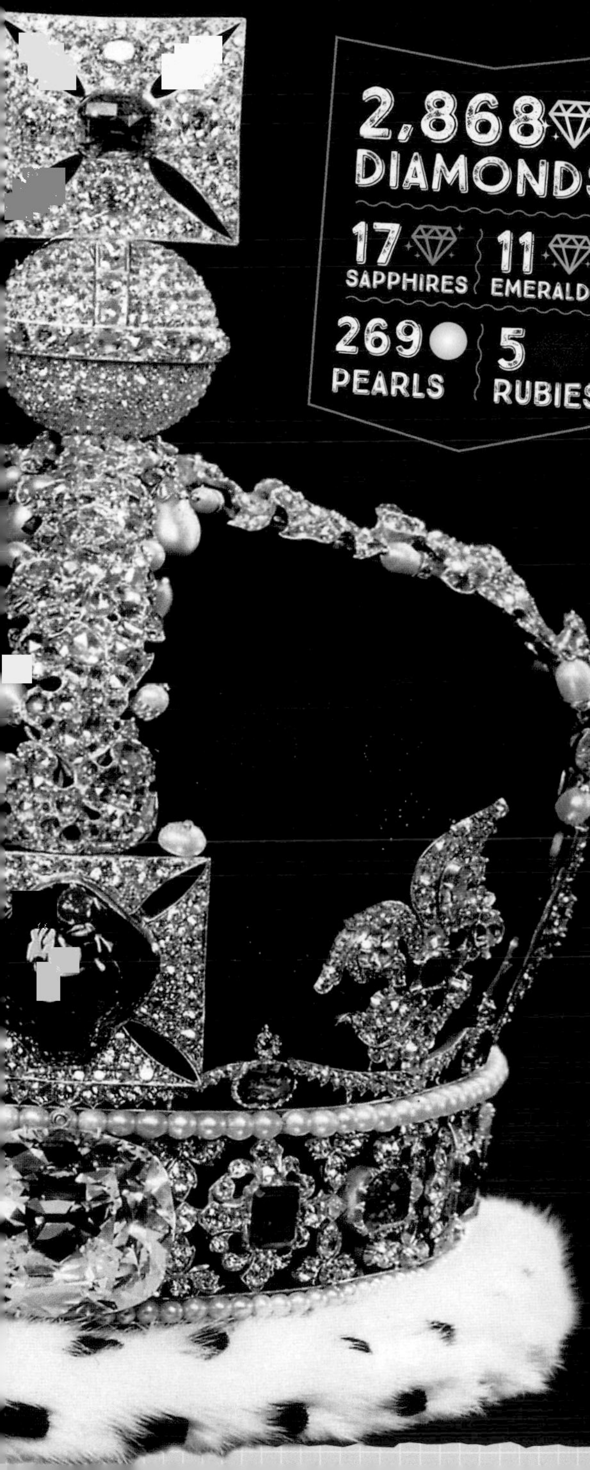

2,868 DIAMONDS

17 SAPPHIRES

11 EMERALDS

269 PEARLS

5 RUBIES

STOLEN!

IN 1671, THOMAS BLOOD AND HIS GANG TRIED TO STEAL THE CROWN JEWELS AND NEARLY GOT AWAY WITH IT. BLOOD TRICKED THE KEEPER OF THE JEWELS INTO LETTING HIM SEE THEM. THEN HE KNOCKED THE KEEPER OUT, FLATTENED EDWARD'S CROWN WITH A MALLET, AND HID IT UNDER HIS CLOAK. HE EVEN STUFFED AN ORB DOWN HIS BREECHES! THE ALARM WAS RAISED JUST IN TIME AND THE GANG WAS CAUGHT.

THE BIGGIE

The top of the scepter is fitted with the largest colorless diamond in the world, the Cullinan I, shown here. It was cut from the biggest diamond ever found, the Cullinan Diamond, which measured nearly 4 inches (10 cm) long. That's over half the size of this book! It was discovered in a South African mine by a mine manager who was walking through a tunnel. He noticed a lump of crystal in the wall and used his cane to pry it out.

WORLD'S BIGGEST DIAMOND!

YUMMY LONDON

London is one of the world's great food capitals. It's chock-full of top restaurants and delicious cafés, some of them serving up some surprising platefuls. Get your knife and fork ready!

*Fragrant as honey
and sweeter in taste!
As flaky and white as
if baked by the light,
As the flesh of an infant
soft, doughy and slight.*

CAPTAIN BUN'S SPICY BITE

CHELSEA

A famous British cake, the Chelsea bun, was first baked in the 1700s and sold in a long-gone shop called the Old Chelsea Bun House. Its owner was nicknamed Captain Bun, and it's said that thousands lined up to taste the spicy fruit buns warm from the oven, including royalty. One local poet got so excited over the buns that he wrote a poem about them (above).

FRUITY MEATY FUN

MANDARIN ORIENTAL HOTEL, KNIGHTSBRIDGE

If top chef Heston Blumenthal ever hands you a juicy-looking orange, be ready for a taste-bud challenge. The "meat fruit," served at his world-famous London restaurant, looks just like an orange but it is actually made of orange jelly with a tasty meaty mixture inside. Heston loves to experiment and come up with recipes for dotty but delicious dishes that surprise everyone.

GOLDEN BITE

HONKY TONK, CHELSEA

In 2014, a London restaurant created the world's most expensive burger, the "Glamburger," costing a tasty US$1,700. It was made of expensive beef wrapped around a piece of black-truffle-flavored Brie cheese, topped with lobster, caviar, maple-glazed bacon, and a gold-leaf-covered duck egg, inside a bun covered in gold leaf. As if that wasn't enough, slivers of white truffle plus champagne sauce went on the plate, too.

TOP TEA

PICCADILLY

FORTNUM & MASON, PICCADILLY

Fortnum & Mason is one of London's poshest grocers. It has sold tea for 300 years, and the tea salon there is a top spot to sip the brew and nibble cucumber sandwiches or jam-slathered scones. The habit of having afternoon tea and cakes caught on in London in the 1800s. It became a grand party event, with people sending invitations to their friends and wearing their best gloves to eat their cakes and sandwiches.

FOUR BEAUTIFUL GILDED BEEHIVES ARE KEPT ON THE ROOF OF FORTNUM & MASON. IN RETURN FOR THEIR LUXURIOUS LIFESTYLE, THE BEES MAKE TOP-QUALITY HONEY FOR THE SHOP'S CUSTOMERS.

DARK DINING

CLERKENWELL GREEN

"Dans le Noir" means "in the dark," so it was a good name to give a restaurant where customers eat in pitch-black surroundings. They aren't told what the food is, so they have to rely on smell, taste, and touch to tell what they're eating. Stemless glasses help to stop them from spilling their drinks, but it's hard to find the cutlery, so diners eat the gourmet feast with their hands. Visually impaired staff members guide the guests around, and the guests leave with a better understanding of what it's like to be blind.

PRECIOUS PARMESAN

SEETHING LANE

London diarist Samuel Pepys was caught up in the Great Fire of London in 1666, and he had to save his most valuable possessions from the fire – including a giant wheel of Parmesan cheese! It was too heavy to carry, so Pepys buried it in his garden. Was he just crazy for cheese? No. He was trying not to lose money. Parmesan cheese was highly prized and very costly in his day. Even today, valuable Parmesans are sometimes stored in bank vaults in Italy.

SEETHING LANE

MAYORAL MOUTHFULS

GUILDHALL AND MANSION HOUSE

GUILDHALL AND MANSION HOUSE

The oldest area in London is known as the City of London and has its own lord mayor. A new lord mayor is appointed every November, when there's a grand feast called the Lord Mayor's Banquet at the Guildhall. It's been held for 800 years.

In December, the lord mayor gets another food treat – a roasted pig's head that has been presented by the Butcher's Company for around 800 years. The butchers march through the stree carrying a giant papier-mâché pig's head to the lord mayor's base at Mansion House. They send the real one on ahead for the lord mayor to enjoy.

R-EEL-Y TASTY

EAST END

EAST END

Jellied eels were once a common food in London's East End, along with pickled cockles and meat pies. The recipe involves chopping eels, boiling them in stock, and allowing the mix to cool and set, forming a jelly around the eels. It is traditionally eaten cold, and it's still served in some East End cafés, where customers can also try stewed eels with a parsley gravy made from the boiled-eel liquid, called liquor.

DOG BISCUITS BEGIN

A SHIPYARD BY THE THAMES

In the 1860s, American electrician James Spratt was going door-to-door in London, trying to sell his services. He saw local dogs eating scraps of hardtack at a shipyard, and it gave him the idea to make the world's first dog biscuits.

THAMES SHIPYARD

GO WILD

Over 8 million people live in London, but nature makes its home here, too. All sorts of amazing animals and extraordinary plants are to be found around town.

KEW'S BIGGEST PITCHER PLANTS ARE CAPABLE OF GOBBLING UP SMALL BIRDS AND MAMMALS.

MEAT-EATING MONSTERS

KEW GARDENS

Kew Gardens was founded in 1840, and is one of the most important plant-studying centers in the world, with a huge collection of plants and trees from around the planet. Many of them have been saved from extinction and are looked after by the brilliant Kew botanists.

1,064,035

The number of names on the Plant List, a record of world plant names compiled by Kew Gardens and the Missouri Botanical Garden.

KEW GARDENS

MURDER!

Kew's Prince of Wales Conservatory is the hottest, most humid greenhouse in Kew, and it's home to meat-eating monsters! Here lurk the pitchers, innocent-looking jug-shaped plants. Inside a pitcher's jug there is sweet nectar to tempt in small creatures, but once a critter gets inside, it's doomed. There is no escape up the plant's steep sides, and the poor creature gets slowly digested by liquid in the plant. The plant feeds on the nutrients from the melted body of its prey.

DEADLIEST EVER

Kew Gardens offers tours and talks about its poisonous plants, but nobody gets to touch! The gardens have two of the most poisonous plants in the world. One seed from the castor oil plant or the strychnine tree could kill an adult human.

WORLD'S WORST STINK

KEW HAS TWO TITUM ARUMS, NICKNAMED CORPSE PLANTS BECAUSE THEIR FLOWERS SMELL LIKE A ROTTING DEAD BODY (THINK OF MEAT THAT'S PAST ITS SELL-BY DATE, AND TRY NOT TO GAG). IT'S THE WORLD'S STINKIEST PLANT SPECIES, BUT LUCKILY IT ONLY FLOWERS EVERY FEW YEARS.

HORRID HELPER

Pinguicula moranensis is a meat-eater that helps out with pest control at Kew. Its round leaves have a slimy, sticky surface that catches flying insects like flypaper. It's especially useful for catching an annoying pest called the sciarid fly, which bothers the botanists because it lays its eggs on plants.

SQUEAKY SPOTTING

LONDON WETLAND CENTRE, BARNES

Seven different species of bat swoop their way through London, and the Wetland Centre in Barnes is one of the best places to see them. Bat fans who visit Barnes are given a detector that picks up the high-pitched signals bats make as they soar and flutter through the twilight sky above. London bats include Britain's smallest bat, the common pipistrelle, which has a wingspan of around 8 inches (20 cm). It's also home to one of Britain's largest bats, the noctule, with a whopping wingspan of 16 inches (40 cm).

LONDON ZOO

FIGHT!

RICHMOND PARK

Richmond Park is the largest enclosed green space in London and it seems an unlikely location for some serious fighting. But red deer and fallow deer have roamed the park for centuries, and each fall the males clash antlers, bellowing and barking loudly. This is rutting season, when they compete for mates. The stags get very pumped up, and visitors are warned to keep their distance.

RICHMOND PARK

CELEBRITY CRITTERS

LONDON ZOO

London Zoo is the world's oldest scientific zoo, founded in 1828. Around 806 species of animals are displayed, studied, and conserved here, and some of them are celebrities. Ricky the Rockhopper penguin is famously the most bad-tempered bird in the penguin pool and has his own fans and Facebook page. Past residents include Guy the Gorilla, a famously gentle beast who cradled birds in his hands, and Goldie the Golden Eagle, who caused London traffic jams during an escape in 1965.

~ RICKY ~

FLEET STREET

When an African grey parrot called Polly died in 1926, it's said that 200 newspapers around the world covered her death. Why was she such a celebrity squawker? Because she lived for 40 years or so at Ye Olde Cheshire Cheese, a pub in Fleet Street, and became world famous for her mimicry, shouting out fake pub orders and cursing terribly. When Princess Mary insisted on meeting her, there was great anxiety that Polly would shock the princess with her rude language, but luckily the conversation stayed polite. Polly still sits in a corner of the pub but she's quiet now, because she's stuffed.

FLEET STREET

TATE MODERN

SPEEDY HUNTERS

TATE MODERN

Peregrine falcons are the fastest creatures on the planet. When they dive down to attack their prey, they can reach an incredible 200 miles per hour (322 km/hr). They like wide open spaces and cliffs, but they occasionally decide to live on city buildings (which are a little bit like cliffs). A few of them have chosen London's Tate Modern art museum (below) as a place to hang out. Sometimes bird-watchers wait outside with their binoculars, hoping for a peek at London's fastest residents.

TOWER OF LONDON

ROYAL BIRDS

TOWER OF LONDON

Ravens have lived at the Tower of London for centuries. Legend has it that if they ever leave, the kingdom will fall, so there are always at least six of them kept at the tower by royal decree. The birds have one wing clipped to stop them from flying off, but they are spoiled rotten, with daily raw meat and blood-soaked cookies. In spite of this, birds do sometimes decide to leave, or behave so badly they have to go. One raven flew off and was last spotted outside a London pub, while another was fired for eating television antennas.

THE GOAT RACE

SPITALFIELDS CITY FARM

You may have heard of the annual Oxford vs. Cambridge Boat Race, when university rowing teams compete along the River Thames. Spitalfields City Farm does its own wild version by playing host to the Oxford vs. Cambridge Goat Race. Goats dressed in university colors run for glory, cheered on by excited crowds. Local people help to run the farm, and it's a popular place to pet a baby pig or learn to spin wool, using wool from the sheep that graze here – just a few lamb skips away from the heart of the city.

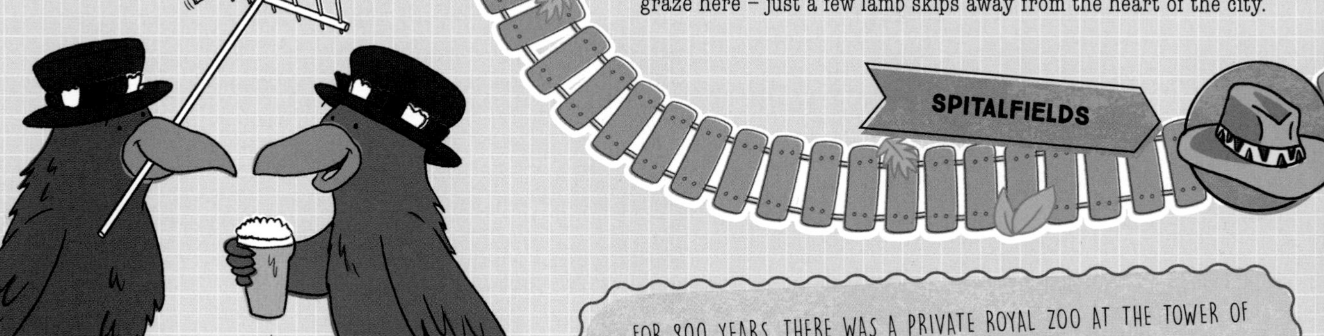

FOR 800 YEARS, THERE WAS A PRIVATE ROYAL ZOO AT THE TOWER OF LONDON. IT WAS HOME TO ALL KINDS OF CRITTERS – EVEN A POLAR BEAR WHO WAS ALLOWED TO FISH IN THE THAMES. THE ZOO IS SHUT NOW, BUT ONE RESIDENT IS STILL RUMORED TO BE PROWLING AROUND. A GRIZZLY BEAR CALLED OLD MARTIN IS SAID TO HAUNT THE TOWER AS A GIANT GROWLING GHOSTIE!

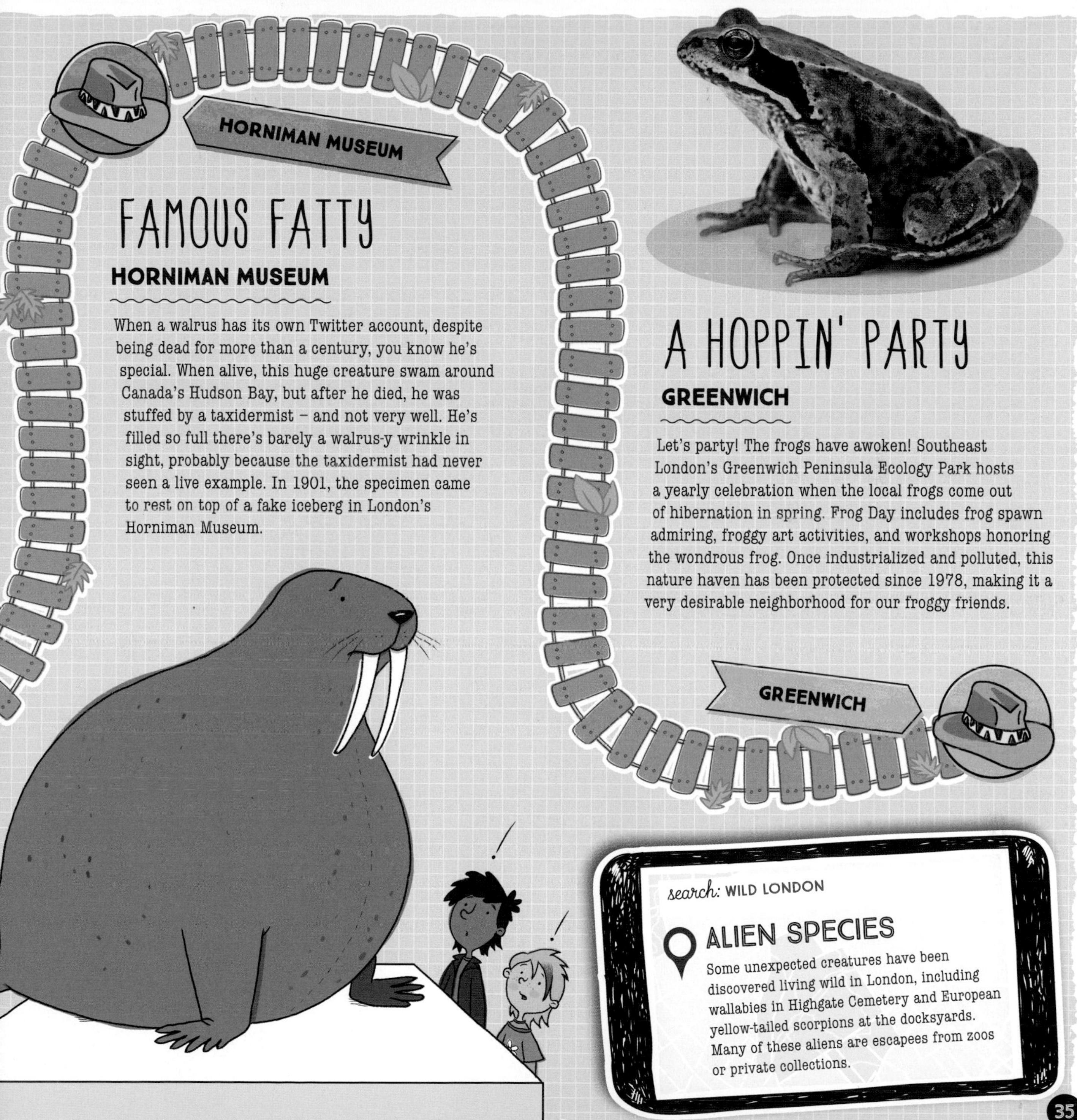

FAMOUS FATTY

HORNIMAN MUSEUM

When a walrus has its own Twitter account, despite being dead for more than a century, you know he's special. When alive, this huge creature swam around Canada's Hudson Bay, but after he died, he was stuffed by a taxidermist – and not very well. He's filled so full there's barely a walrus-y wrinkle in sight, probably because the taxidermist had never seen a live example. In 1901, the specimen came to rest on top of a fake iceberg in London's Horniman Museum.

A HOPPIN' PARTY

GREENWICH

Let's party! The frogs have awoken! Southeast London's Greenwich Peninsula Ecology Park hosts a yearly celebration when the local frogs come out of hibernation in spring. Frog Day includes frog spawn admiring, froggy art activities, and workshops honoring the wondrous frog. Once industrialized and polluted, this nature haven has been protected since 1978, making it a very desirable neighborhood for our froggy friends.

search: WILD LONDON

ALIEN SPECIES

Some unexpected creatures have been discovered living wild in London, including wallabies in Highgate Cemetery and European yellow-tailed scorpions at the docksyards. Many of these aliens are escapees from zoos or private collections.

MAGICAL MYSTERIES AND LEGENDS

Follow this enchanted trail to discover the magicians, spells, and legends that have touched London with their magic and mystery!

KENSINGTON GARDENS

THE FAIRY BOY

PETER PAN, KENSINGTON GARDENS

In 1912, J. M. Barrie, author of the famous children's book *Peter Pan*, commissioned a statue of Peter, which stands in Kensington Gardens. In Barrie's story, Peter Pan is a boy who never grows up, and he leads a crew of young mischief-makers, the Lost Boys, through adventures with fairies, mermaids, and pirates. Little fairies, rabbits, squirrels, and mice climb around Peter's statue, which is on the exact spot where he landed after flying out of a nursery window in the story.

PETER PAN HAS COME UP-TO-DATE. VISITORS CAN SWIPE A SMARTPHONE ACROSS A PLAQUE NEAR THE STATUE AND GET A PERSONAL CALL FROM PETER HIMSELF!

THE CLEVEREST CAT IN TOWN

WHITTINGTON'S CAT, HIGHGATE HILL

The legend of London hero Dick Whittington rests on his cat. This feisty feline sailed on a ship to a faraway country and killed all the rats there. The country's emperor paid Dick lots of money for his clever cat's services, making his fortune. There's a statue of the cat at Highgate Hill, where Dick is said to have stood and listened to London's church bells calling him back when he was about to give up on the city and leave.

HIGHGATE HILL

MAGICIAN CENTRAL

MAGIC CIRCLE HEADQUARTERS

Picture a magician on stage, and you probably see someone in a long cape and top hat, sawing his assistant in half. This type of magic act was developed in London in the 1800s, when illusionists pioneered many new tricks, such as appearing to float, escaping from handcuffs, and pretending to carry their head under their arm. British magicians were fearful that the secrets of their trade would be discovered, so they set up a society of magicians, the Magic Circle, in 1905. The Magic Circle has its own museum and a Young Magician's Club for budding trick-masters.

POTTER SPOTTER

KING'S CROSS STATION AND OTHER POTTER SPOTS

Fictional boy wizard Harry Potter traveled to his magical school at Hogwarts from platform 9¾ at King's Cross Station. Harry had to ram his luggage cart against a wall, but the kind folks at the station have embedded a cart in the wall near platform 9 so that Potter fans can re-enact the scene without breaking their nose on the brick. There are several other London locations for Potter-spotters, too. Harry learned to speak Parseltongue at London Zoo's Reptile House, and the inspiration for Diagon Alley is said to be somewhere near Charing Cross Road. Leadenhall Market was the location for Diagon Alley in the *Philosopher's Stone* movie.

MYSTERY MAN

LUDGATE

A truly mysterious story grew up around a mythical founder of London called King Lud. Legend has it that Lud's family fought against the Romans when they invaded, and that Lud loved the city so much, he built an entrance to it at Ludgate. There is no King Lud in British history, and the truth behind this myth is lost in the mists of time, so why not make up your own version? Statues of King Lud and his sons stand outside St. Dunstan-in-the-West church, so you could use them as your London Lud story inspiration.

CANNON STREET

SYMBOLIC STONE

CANNON STREET

A large stone sits by the side of a busy London street, and many people pass it by without a glance. Yet if legend is to be believed, it is the key to London's fate! It's called the London Stone, and the story goes that if it is ever destroyed, the city will go, too. It was once very famous, and people were obsessed by its magical power. Some said it came from an ancient sacred altar, others that it was the stone that once held King Arthur's sword Excalibur. The truth? Who knows!

MESSY MITHRAS

MUSEUM OF LONDON

The Ancient Romans lived in Londinium (their name for London) for nearly 2,000 years. Many Roman soldiers worshipped a god called Mithras, and in 1954, the remains of a temple dedicated to Mithras were found in the City of London. Artifacts including the carving below were discovered in the mud and are now in the Museum of London. Worshippers of Mithras held weird initiation ceremonies in their temples. It's said they stood under a grating while a bull was sacrificed above them, drenching them in its blood.

MUSEUM OF LONDON

search: TEMPLE OF MITHRAS

400,000

The number of people who lined up in just two weeks to see the newly discovered Temple of Mithras in 1954.

WHEN GIANTS RULED

THE GUILDHALL

Two magical giants live at the Guildhall in the City of London! The legend goes that long, long ago, Britain was a land called Albion, where a fearsome race of giants lived. Two of them, Gog and Magog, were defeated by a hero called Brutus and chained to the gates of his palace, said to be on the spot where the Guildhall now sits. Carvings of the giants are kept in the Guildhall, and every year giant models of Gog and Magog lead the procession for the Lord Mayor's Show, when the lord mayor travels through town.

LONDON WHEELS

Getting around the roads of busy London can take a while, but you don't need to wait. This route is just for you, and there are no traffic jams – only amazing facts at every stop! Take a seat on the Lonely Planet ride and enjoy.

START

SOUTH KENSINGTON

PARKED IN THE PARK

LONDON TO BRIGHTON VINTAGE CAR RUN, HYDE PARK START

At sunrise on the first Sunday in November, 500 or so vintage vehicles fire up their engines in Hyde Park. It's the start of the world's oldest motoring event, and the oily oldsters hope to make their way from London to the Brighton seafront 60 miles (95.5 km) away. Before the event begins, a red flag is ceremonially destroyed in the park. That's because the first race in 1896 celebrated the end of an early motoring law insisting that a man had to walk in front of a car, waving a red warning flag!

OLD TREASURE OF A TRAIN

SCIENCE MUSEUM, SOUTH KENSINGTON

Meet the world's oldest surviving steam locomotive, Puffing Billy. He was built in 1814 to haul coal wagons all the way from a mine to the dockyards in Northumberland. Instead of two horse-drawn wagons a day, Puffing Billy could drag up to 12 wagons an hour – quite a breakthrough. No wonder he remained in use until 1862.

HYDE PARK

TOP HATS AND TITTLE-TATTLE

ROTTEN ROW, HYDE PARK

Before newspapers and the Internet, Londoners got their celebrity gossip from riding along Rotten Row – once THE place to be seen in London. It's a track from Hyde Park Corner to Serpentine Road, where well-heeled 18th- and 19th-century Londoners would ride their horses or sit in horse-drawn carriages, showing off in their finest clothes and flirting. There were strict speed limits, which allowed plenty of time to ogle each other. Royal princes and their girlfriends were sometimes to be seen here, creating a galloping rumor mill of gossip.

HYDE PARK

COSY FOR CABMEN

WEST LONDON

Dotted around West London there are reminders of times gone by, when Victorian cabbies drove horse-drawn cabs around the city. Drivers had to sit on the top of their cab in all kinds of weather, so it's not surprising they liked to take a break every now and then. The trouble was, they tended to go to the pub... which wasn't great for road safety. So a society was set up to build shelters where cab drivers could warm up with a hot drink and a snack – not alcohol. These saintly shacks look a bit like garden sheds on the side of the road. There are about a dozen still surviving around Chelsea, Kensington, and Westminster.

LOST IN LONDON

200 BAKER STREET

200 Baker Street is London Transport's lost and found. Over the years, people have left some pretty weird stuff on the capital's buses, trains, motor coaches, and taxis, and it all ends up here. Valuable items get auctioned off if they are unclaimed.

Items lost over the years include:

- ➡ COFFIN (A THEATER PROP)
- ➡ TWO HUMAN SKULLS
- ➡ STUFFED EAGLE
- ➡ DRIED PUFFER FISH
- ➡ GARDEN BENCH
- ➡ CHILDREN'S SLIDE
- ➡ DIVING HARPOON
- ➡ GRANDFATHER CLOCK
- ➡ 14-FOOT (4 M) BOAT

BAKER STREET

RECORD WHEELS

THE LONDON WHEELCHAIR MARATHON, HORSE GUARDS PARADE (START AND FINISH)

The London Marathon has been run alongside the River Thames since 1981 and it's globally famous, but the London Wheelchair Marathon is arguably even more exciting to watch. Rules stipulate no electric wheelchairs, and participants must be able to propel themselves along, so there's no souping up your wheelchair before you join in.

HORSE GUARDS PARADE

ALL ABOARD

LONDON TRANSPORT MUSEUM, COVENT GARDEN

All aboard for a trip through London's wheely interesting history. This transportation-themed museum showcases the ways people have traveled around London for over two centuries, from sedan chairs and a horse-drawn bus to the first underground engine, which was steam-powered. Visitors get to sit in the cab of a red bus and drive a Tube train on a Northern Line Underground simulator.

SEDAN CHAIRS WERE USED IN LONDON IN THE 18TH CENTURY. THEY WERE CARRIED BY TWO STRONG MEN – ONE AT THE FRONT AND ONE AT THE BACK. INSIDE, THERE WAS ENOUGH ROOM TO SQUEEZE IN THE FANCY WIGS AND GOWNS WORN AT THE TIME. SEDAN CHAIR MEN WERE NOTORIOUS FOR THEIR TERRIBLE SWEARING, THOUGH!

COVENT GARDEN

SHOREDITCH

PEDAL PARTY

SHOREDITCH

The Pedibus is London's bar on wheels. It trundles through the streets, powered by the legs of its patrons. Up to 12 people can sit on board the Pedibus and pedal their way around London while having a party.

EVERYWHERE!

BRILLIANT BUSES

THE LONDON BUS

EVERYONE knows about London's bright red buses. They're famous the world over, so there's no way we could have a bus-free book. Here's one now. Hop on!

THE ICONIC ONE

The iconic London bus is the double-decker, rear-doored Routemaster model. It was replaced in 2005 by more modern buses, but there are quite a few still around, either on display or running on popular tourist routes and making everyone feel nostalgic.

PILFERED FROM PARIS

The very first London "omnibus" ran in 1829 between Paddington and Bank. It held 22 passengers and was pulled by three horses. The man who set it up, George Shillibeer, stole the idea from Paris.

WHY RED?

Before 1907, there were lots of different-colored buses run by different companies. A company called London General Omnibus Company painted theirs red to stand out from the crowd, and it must have worked because they soon became the biggest bus operator in town.

HOW GHOSTS GET AROUND

A PHANTOM NUMBER 7 GHOST BUS IS OCCASIONALLY SAID TO APPEAR IN THE MIDDLE OF THE NIGHT IN CAMBRIDGE GARDENS, WITH NO DRIVER AND NO LIGHTS. OUR ADVICE? DO NOT GET ON THIS ONE!

FUTURE BUS

Nowadays, London's buses have hi-tech GPS satellite tracking on board, and you can watch them moving around on a virtual map of London's streets.

The future is looking even brighter for them. Red buses are going green, with trials of zero-emissions electric buses starting.

NO KIDDING!

Daredevil motorcycle stunt riders love to jump over London double-decker buses, and you can see them in online video clips. Stunt star Eddie Kidd once jumped over 14!

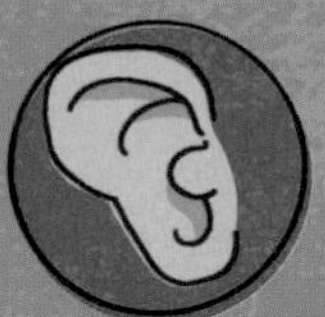

LONDON OUT LOUD

London has many famous landmarks and streets, but how about following some of its sounds instead? Keep your ears open on this trail to hear some of the sounds around town.

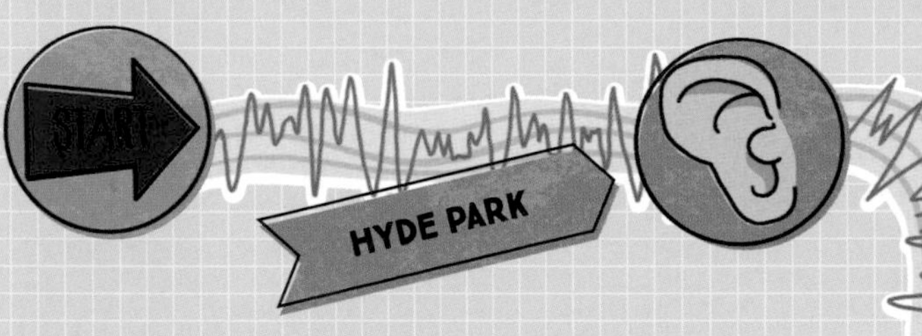

AND ANOTHER THING...

SPEAKERS' CORNER

This corner of Hyde Park is the place to come to hear people making speeches. Anyone can turn up unannounced to give a talk here, as long as what they say doesn't break the law of the land. All kinds of ranting goes on, and it's often been the site of rallies and protests. Criminals were once hanged near this spot, at Tyburn Gallows, and before they died, they were allowed to say whatever final words they wanted. That's probably why this area has stayed such a hotspot for free speech.

BANGIN' BIRTHDAYS

HYDE PARK, GREEN PARK, TOWER OF LONDON

On official royal celebration days, such as royal birthdays, cannon salutes fired from Hyde Park, Green Park, or the Tower of London ring out across London. A 21-gun salute is traditional in Britain, but London does things bigger! In the royal parks, another 20 rounds are added, and 41 rounds are fired. At the Tower of London, 62 rounds are fired on royal anniversaries – and sometimes even an ear-shattering 124 rounds!

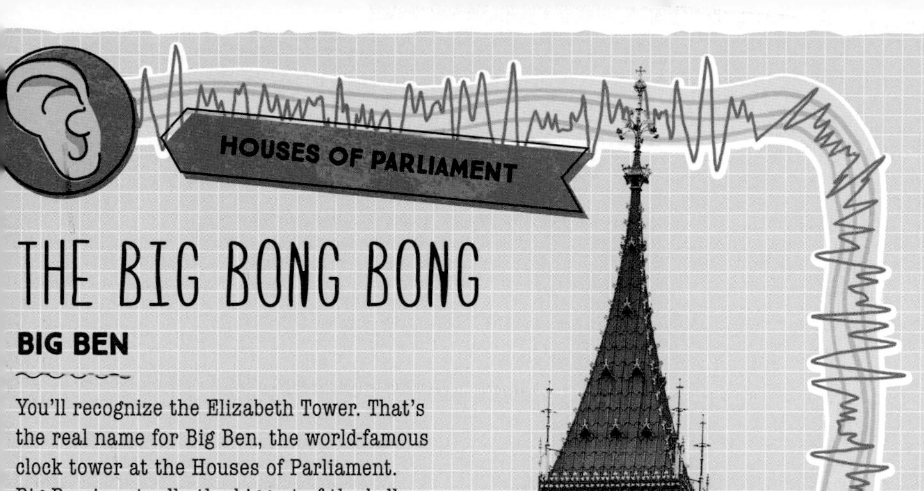

THE BIG BONG BONG

BIG BEN

You'll recognize the Elizabeth Tower. That's the real name for Big Ben, the world-famous clock tower at the Houses of Parliament. Big Ben is actually the biggest of the bells inside, which first chimed in 1859. It weighs as much as a small elephant, and when it was first made, 16 horses were needed to haul it through London to the tower. Londoners soon nicknamed it, but no one is sure why. It could be after the man who oversaw its installation, or after a well-known boxing champ at the time. Big Ben's first chime marks each hour and is accurate to within a second.

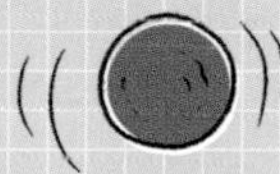

23 FT. (7 M)
WIDTH OF CLOCK DIALS

2 FT. (60 CM)
HEIGHT OF CLOCK NUMBERS

14 FT. (4.2 M)
MINUTE-HAND LENGTH

9 FT. (2.7 M)
HOUR-HAND LENGTH

NOISIEST SPOTS IN TOWN

TOTTENHAM COURT ROAD

Where are London's noise hotspots? Here are the top three notoriously noisy places, according to a study done in 2010.

1. Tottenham Court Road

94.9 DECIBELS
With traffic streaming along it all day, the noise on the street can reach volumes as loud as a plane landing.

2. Charing Cross Tube station

89.9 DECIBELS
Like standing about 3 feet (1 m) away from a pneumatic drill.

3. Covent Garden

81.5 DECIBELS
Like standing next to a ringing phone.

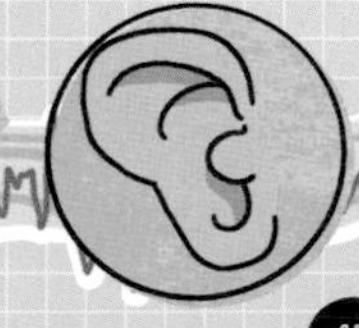

SYMBOL OF HOPE

The sound of Bow Bells meant so much to Londoners that the BBC World Service broadcast a recording of them pealing on the radio, as a symbol of hope during World War II.

LULLABY FACTORY

GREAT ORMOND STREET HOSPITAL

The Lullaby Factory is a secret soundscape hidden inside Great Ormond Street Hospital for Children. Inside the building complex, there's a courtyard where a ten-story installation of amazing pipes produces soothing lullabies that can be heard through pipes at its base, or by tuning in to a special hospital radio frequency. Architects decided to make a feature of the ugly pipes on the building and created this imaginative work for the kids staying in the hospital.

LISTEN OUT FOR LONDONERS

BOW BELLS

It's said that to be a cockney (a true Londoner) you need to be born within earshot of Bow Bells – the bell peal of St. Mary-le-Bow church in Cheapside, East London. The bells ring every 15 minutes, but traffic and aircraft noise have made the sound much harder to hear these days, and there are no maternity wards in the area where the bells can be heard any more. Luckily, concerned cockneys can download a recording of the bells to play wherever they happen to be having their babies.

RECORD-BREAKING ROCKERS

THE VALLEY (CHARLTON ATHLETIC FOOTBALL STADIUM)

Rock bands make London's loudest noises and have occasionally broken world records. In 1972, Deep Purple became the loudest band in the world when their show at London's Rainbow Theatre reached 117 decibels (three audience members were knocked unconscious by the sound). The Who bust the record (and possibly some eardrums) in 1976 with a performance registering 126 decibels at the Valley, Charlton Athletic's soccer stadium. The official "threshold of pain" for tolerating loud sounds is 120 decibels, so that music must have hurt! Maybe people are getting more tolerant (or deaf).

ST. PAUL'S CATHEDRAL

THE VALLEY FOOTBALL GROUND

BIG LITTLE VOICES

ST. PAUL'S CATHEDRAL

For 900 years or more, boys have been singing in the world-renowned choir at St. Paul's Cathedral. The young choristers go to boarding school at St. Paul's Cathedral School. They rehearse every day before class, and sing most days in the services, as well as on special occasions such as the Lord Mayor's Banquet. Any boy with a good voice can audition to be a St. Paul's chorister. Girls who want to become choristers can join the choir at Southwark Cathedral.

SCREAM STREETS

This trail will lead you past the spooky, the grisly, and the downright dreadful. Be brave. Make sure your stomach is feeling strong, and don't turn around if you hear any footsteps behind you!

HIGHGATE CEMETERY

SPOOKY SPOT

HIGHGATE CEMETERY

In the 1800s, London's burial grounds were overcrowded, and bodies were being stacked on top of each other, not far from the surface. The stench could be terrible, and diseases spread from these sickening sites, so Parliament passed a new law to open some big new cemeteries, including one at Highgate. It's a peaceful spot with many grand tombs, but it's also said to be one of the most haunted places in town – perhaps because it looks like the shivery, spidery set of a Halloween movie at night!

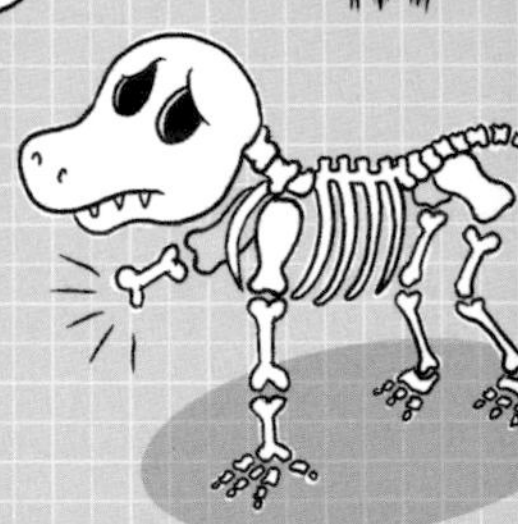

NO MORE WALKS

HYDE PARK PET CEMETERY

This pint-sized cemetery is the final resting place of around 300 pets, buried over a hundred years ago. The first animal to be buried there was a dog called Cherry. Soon, all kinds of pets joined her – some with sweet names, such as Flossie, Lulu, Topper, and Tiddles, and others with more unusual names, like Scum, Smut, Drag, Bogey Church, and Lord Quex. If you ever meet a nighttime spook here, you could probably just tell it to "sit."

HYDE PARK PET CEMETERY

SOUTHWARK

GROANS GUARANTEED

THE HUNTERIAN MUSEUM, LINCOLN'S INN FIELDS

This museum of surgery has a collection groaning with pickled organs, deformed skulls, and weird-looking body parts, all collected by surgeons over the years. Horrible highlights include the skeleton of a giant man who was 7 feet 7 inches (2.3 m) tall, a necklace made of human teeth, and a selection of seriously scary-looking surgical instruments guaranteed to make visitors wince.

THE HUNTERIAN MUSEUM

GRIM GHOSTS

THE CLINK PRISON, SOUTHWARK

Even today British people refer to going to jail as being thrown in "the Clink," and this grim prison is where the phrase began. Unlucky inmates passed through this miserable place from the 1100s, accused of anything from ghastly murders to a debt of a few pounds. If you think being locked up here and weighed down with irons was bad enough, just wait until they bring out the torture devices...

It's now a museum, but at night it's said to be heavily haunted, and some peculiar people are crazy enough to have sleepovers here!

OUCH!

OLD OPERATING THEATRE, ST. THOMAS STREET

Finding yourself on this wooden table was bad news, especially when someone brought out the saw. Trainee doctors used to cram into this 150-year-old operating theater to observe unfortunate patients having their limbs hacked off! It was shut in 1862 and forgotten, then rediscovered when someone decided to explore the attic of St. Thomas's Hospital.

HERBS HIGH UP

ST. THOMAS'S HOSPITAL WAS SET UP NEARLY 1,000 YEARS AGO. IN THE 1600S, AN ATTIC ROOM WAS CREATED IN THE RAFTERS ABOVE THE HOSPITAL CHURCH. HERE, APOTHECARIES MADE MEDICINES USING HERBS, AND IT'S OPEN TO VISITORS TODAY. SOME OF THEIR WEIRD "CURES" ARE RECORDED IN OLD HOSPITAL RECORDS. IF YOU WERE ILL IN 1603, FOR EXAMPLE, YOU MIGHT HAVE A BATH OF HERBS AND SHEEP'S HEADS, OR AN OINTMENT MIXED FROM HERBS, GOOSE FAT, HONEY, AND DUNG.

CHOPPING SPOT

At some point, a ward for sick women was created, and this is where things get gruesome. Operations were done in the ward with the other poor patients looking on! Thankfully, in 1822, the operating theater was moved away from the patients, and this little room is what visitors can see today – along with a display of preserved body parts and horrid-looking surgical tools, such as a "tonsil guillotine," eye scalpels, and amputation saws. There are even helpful amputation diagrams on the walls.

MESSY MINUTE

When operations were performed, there was no anesthetic, only some strong alcohol to help dull the pain. Surgeons had to be quick, and the best ones could cut off a limb in a minute – but there would have been lots of blood. A box of sawdust was kept under the operating table and moved around to catch the gore as it dripped down. The surgeons wore top hats and frock coats.

SLIMY SUCKERS

Leech bowls are on display here, too. These once held slimy black leeches looking for a meal of blood. It was thought that bloodletting (getting rid of some blood) would cure most things, so bloodsucking leeches were regularly attached to patients. Leeches are actually used safely in medicine today, but back then they were not used properly or hygienically, and could make things much, much worse.

LONDON BRIDGE

HEADS UP

LONDON BRIDGE

The lovely view of the River Thames from London Bridge was once spoiled by a ghoulish sight at its southern gatehouse. The heads of traitors were impaled on spikes here and left out for all to see. If you think the heads wouldn't last outdoors, you're wrong. They were first boiled and dipped in tar so they could stay on show for a long time. Guy Fawkes, who was part of a plot to blow up the Houses of Parliament, was one of the traitors who "headed" this way, in 1606.

HOXTON STREET

SHOPPING FOR SPOOKS

HOXTON STREET MONSTER SUPPLIES

If you're a zombie, werewolf, or vampire and can't find a store that suits your shopping needs, here's the hilarious answer! Hoxton Street Monster Supplies is stocked with everyday items for the undead. Goods found on the shelves include cans of panic and fear, jars of snot, brain jam, and salt made from tears. All the profits go to a charity that supports kids' creative writing.

GRISLY WARNING

EXECUTION DOCK, WAPPING

For more than 400 years, pirates were hanged at Wapping's Execution Dock. They were hanged at low tide, then left to be washed by the river for a day or two before being cut down and buried in an unmarked grave. The most notorious individuals were covered in tar after their death and hanged in chains in an iron cage, for all the locals to see as they rotted away. It was a grisly warning for others to behave. Infamous pirate Captain Kidd was hanged here, then chained in an iron cage at nearby Tilbury, where every passing ship could catch sight of him.

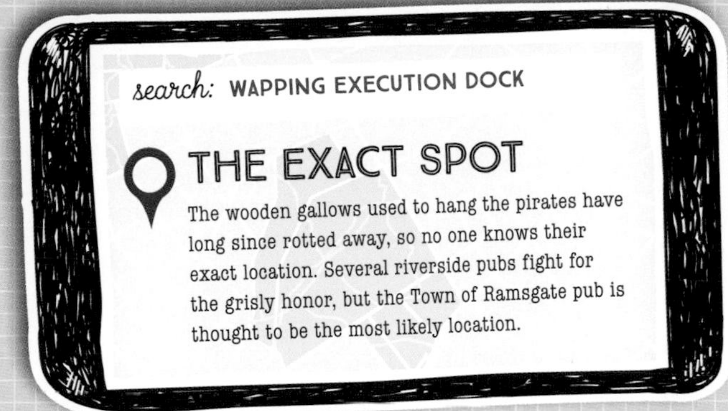

THE EXACT SPOT

The wooden gallows used to hang the pirates have long since rotted away, so no one knows their exact location. Several riverside pubs fight for the grisly honor, but the Town of Ramsgate pub is thought to be the most likely location.

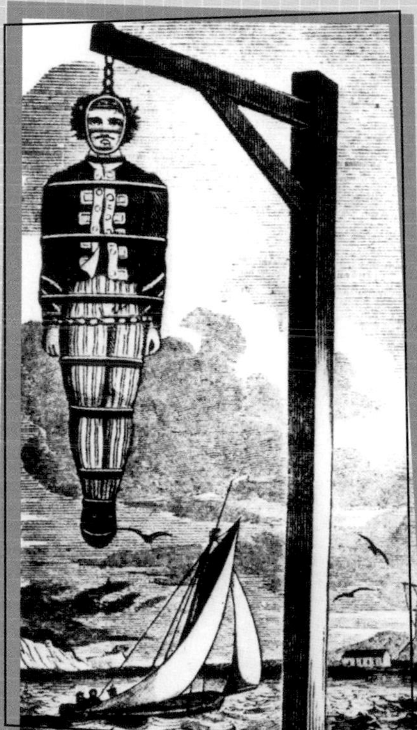

SHADWELL

BURIED BODIES

ST. PAUL'S CHURCH, SHADWELL

Throughout history, London has been regularly hit by deadly epidemics, including the terrifying plague, carried by rats, which struck repeatedly in medieval times and again in 1664, when around 70,000 people died. It was a problem knowing where to bury all the bodies, so huge plague pits were dug and piled with corpses. Plague pit sites are all over London, and are often rediscovered on building sites. There are thought to be at least five plague pits in Shadwell, where the disease quickly ripped through the slums.

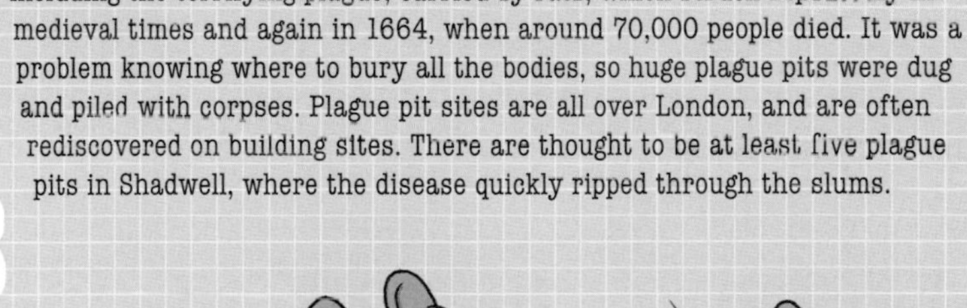

HEY, BUSYBODY!

Let's peek into some homes around London to see what we can discover. Hopefully nobody will mind if we do a bit of snooping around these amazing abodes to find out a bit more about city life.

BREATHE IN

SHEPHERD'S BUSH

Hold your breath for London's narrowest house, measuring a tiny 6 feet (1.8 m) wide. A grown man could lie down with his head and feet touching the walls on either side, yet this quirky residence has a price tag of around US$796,000! Somehow, they've crammed in seven rooms.

DOOR TO NOWHERE

23–24 LEINSTER TERRACE, BAYSWATER

Two stylish townhouses near Paddington have a surprise secret. They're fake! If you walk around the back and peer over the wall, you'll discover that the house fronts are just a flat façade hiding a secret entrance to the London Underground. The houses were knocked down to build the train track and never rebuilt. In the 1930s, an enterprising prankster sold expensive tickets for a ball at Leinster Gardens, and when guests showed up in their ballgowns, they discovered they were knocking on a door to nowhere.

MEGA-MONEY LIVING

HYDE PARK

In 2014, Number 1 Hyde Park became London's most expensive penthouse apartment. It sold for a mind-boggling US$213 million, working out at around US$8,000 for an area the size of a tablet computer. The weighty price tag also paid for a secret passageway to the Mandarin Oriental Hotel, which has one of the city's most luxurious restaurants.

HYDE PARK

HE LIVED HERE, OR DID HE?

BAKER STREET

Sherlock Holmes, the world-famous detective, lived at 221b Baker Street. Inside, the rooms are filled with his Victorian belongings, including his hat, pipes, violin, and all the equipment he needed for solving mysteries. But wait a minute... Sherlock Holmes never existed! He was an imaginary character in books written by Sir Arthur Conan Doyle. So how come there is a "Sherlock Holmes lived here" plaque on the wall outside his "home"? Mystery solved! It's a museum home based on the books.

BRUNSWICK SQUARE

HEARTBREAKING HOME

FOUNDLING MUSEUM, BRUNSWICK SQUARE

In the 1700s, very poor moms brought their babies here to be looked after and adopted. Each mom left behind a small scrap of fabric, in case she was ever able to return to take her child back. She could then match the fabric with a scrap of her own and prove who she was. The babies were fostered and educated, then sent to work for someone when they were ten.

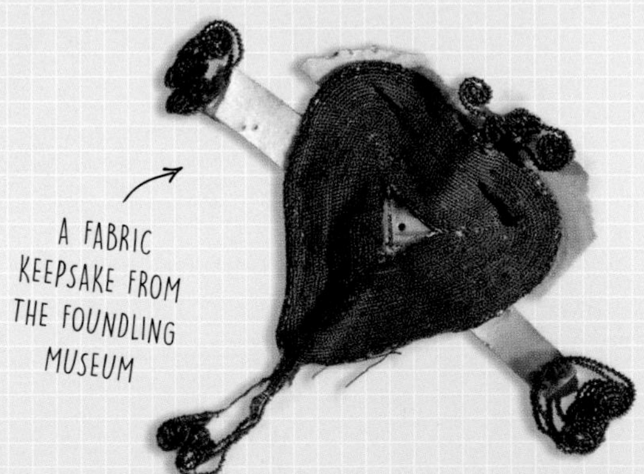

A FABRIC KEEPSAKE FROM THE FOUNDLING MUSEUM

LONDON WRITTEN HERE

DOUGHTY STREET

Charles Dickens was one of London's greatest writers, and here at Doughty Street, he wrote some of his best-loved London stories, such as *Oliver Twist*. Visitors to his Victorian home can see his chair, his writing desk, and even his bedroom. Dickens was a very bad sleeper, though, and often spent nights outdoors, wandering around London's streets looking for inspiration for his tales.

SOME OF THE FAMOUS NOVELS WRITTEN BY CHARLES DICKENS:

- GREAT EXPECTATIONS
- OLIVER TWIST
- NICHOLAS NICKLEBY
- OUR MUTUAL FRIEND
- DAVID COPPERFIELD
- LITTLE DORRIT
- A CHRISTMAS CAROL

DOUGHTY STREET

PLACE FOR THE POOR

RAGGED SCHOOL MUSEUM, TOWER HAMLETS

For centuries, many Londoners lived in great poverty, and poor children went to work, not school. But in Victorian times, a few children got the chance to learn in Ragged Schools – so named because the pupils were dressed in rags. An old Ragged School is now a museum in Hackney. The pupils here would have lived in crowded slums, so perhaps their school was a welcome place to be. The teachers were very strict, though. They sometimes gave pupils dunce caps to wear and beat them for disobedience!

A HOUSE IN TIME

SPITALFIELDS

Dennis Severs' House on Folgate Street is nearly 300 years old, and ten of its rooms are set up as a museum to show how Londoners lived in the 1700s and 1800s. Each room was re-created by artist Dennis Severs to make it seem as if the family who lives in the house has just stepped out of sight. There are unmade beds, partly eaten meals, and the sounds of footsteps and whispers.

TALES OF TAILS

Lots of surprising monsters and big beasties are living around town. Here's a trail to help you discover where dragons, dinosaurs, sea monsters, lions, and... em... a yale are hiding.

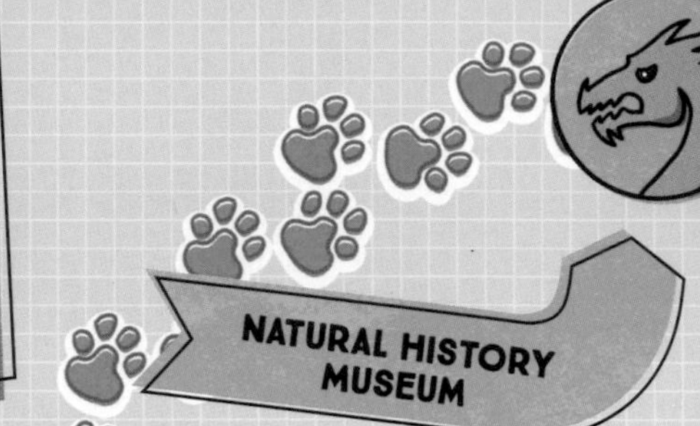

BRIDGE BEASTIES

HAMPTON COURT PALACE

There's a mighty menagerie of monsters on a bridge over the moat at the palace of Hampton Court. Animals have been used for centuries as symbols for aristocratic families, and these ten beautiful beasties represent the various family connections of Tudor King Henry VIII and his third wife, Jane Seymour. There are three lions, two dragons, a bull, a greyhound, a panther, a unicorn, and a yale – a strange medieval monster with the body of an antelope, the tail of an elephant, and the jaws of a boar.

DINOSAUR ROAR

NATURAL HISTORY MUSEUM

Dinosaurs, the original mega-mean monsters, stomped the Earth millions of years ago, and they're still lurking in London. The Natural History Museum's world-renowned dinosaur gallery hosts reconstructed skeletons of some of these fearsome creatures, and life-size animatronic dinos that roar at visitors as they walk past. Particularly terrifying is the T-rex that lurks in a swampy pit, sensing passers-by and baring teeth 6 inches (15 cm) long as it sizes them up as prey!

SCARY SCULPTURE

MARBLE ARCH

Modern sculptures pop up regularly around the Westminster area of town, and in 2015, Marble Arch became home to one of the scariest creatures ever seen in the city! *She Guardian*, by Dashi Namdakov, is a cross between a cat, a dragon, and your worst monster nightmares. It's 36 feet (11 m) tall and is designed as a symbol of a mother protecting her young. Come to think of it, moms can get pretty fierce...

LUCKY DANCERS

CHINATOWN

Chinatown is the hub of the Chinese community in London, and when Chinese New Year comes along, dragons and lions dance through the streets here. Chinese dragons are not like scary fire-breathing European dragons. They have stag horns, fish scales, and tiger paws, and they are said to bring good luck. The longer the dragon, the more luck it brings with it.

search: NATURAL HISTORY MUSEUM

DINOSAUR DREAMS

Groups of dinosaur enthusiasts can arrange to have a sleepover at the Natural History Museum and take part in a flashlight tour of the dinosaur gallery. Let's hope they don't have nightmares!

THESE FOUR DON'T ROAR

TRAFALGAR SQUARE

Four famous lion statues are favorites with tourists wanting to take a typical London photo in Trafalgar Square. These big cats guard Nelson's Column, erected to celebrate British naval hero Admiral Lord Nelson.

WRONG LIONS

Nelson's Column appeared in 1843, but the bronze lions didn't arrive until 25 years later. At first, four stone lions were made, but they were rejected for not being grand enough. They were bought by a Victorian factory owner called Titus Salt and they now live in the Yorkshire village of Saltaire, which he built.

WRONG PAWS

Victorian artist Sir Edwin Landseer was commissioned to design grander lions, but it took him nine years to create them. He visited London Zoo to watch the lions there and asked if he could have a dead one to keep in his studio. It took years for a lion to die but eventually he got one. He started to make models of it, but the body began to rot before he could finish so he had to improvise the final details, which is why the lions have the paws of a house cat and not a lion.

BATTLE BRONZE

THE BRONZE USED TO MAKE THE LIONS CAME FROM MELTED CANNONS CAPTURED FROM FRENCH AND SPANISH SHIPS AT THE BATTLE OF TRAFALGAR – NELSON'S GREATEST VICTORY. NELSON'S FORCES BEAT NAPOLÉON IN A SEA BATTLE, BUT NELSON PAID WITH HIS LIFE WHEN HE WAS SHOT BY A FRENCH SNIPER ON THE DECK OF HIS SHIP. HIS STATUE STANDS ON TOP OF THE COLUMN, MINUS AN EYE AND AN ARM, WHICH HE LOST DURING HIS FIGHTING CAREER.

WHO'S WHO?

The lions are "couchant," which is the correct term for their sitting position. They're not all exactly the same, though. Although they have the same pose, their faces and manes are very slightly different.

HEIGHT 11 FT. 3.4 M

LENGTH 20 FT. 6.1 M

EACH LION IS MADE OF 27 DIFFERENT PARTS RIVETED TOGETHER

27

ALIVE!

As part of a publicity stunt in 2015, speakers were hidden behind the lions so that passers-by would think they were roaring loudly and coming to life!

WEIRD WALRUS

ST. PANCRAS

Archaeologists were very confused when the bones of a Pacific walrus were unearthed in a coffin on a St. Pancras building site. The weird walrus remains came to light when a churchyard was being excavated to make way for the Eurostar train terminal. Even more strange, pieces of a tortoise were found, too, and experts began to suspect a grisly secret. It's now thought that the creatures were probably used for medical research in Victorian times, because they were buried along with a number of human bones that had been chopped up.

DRAGON TOWN

CITY OF LONDON

The City of London's symbol is the dragon – and that's why there are so many of these magical beasts infesting the capital! The boundaries of the city are guarded by silver dragons standing on plinths, with upswept wings and pointed tongues, holding shields and swords. The original inspiration for these boundary dragons can be found on the Victoria Embankment, where two dragon specimens 7 feet (2.1 m) tall rear up on their hind legs, grasping the city's coat of arms in their claws.

THERE ARE BEASTS ON THE COUNCIL OF NEARLY EVERY LONDON BOROUGH (OFFICIAL AREA)! EACH BOROUGH HAS ITS OWN COAT OF ARMS AND MANY OF THEM SHOW MYTHICAL BEASTS, INCLUDING LIONS, GRIFFINS, DRAGONS, STAGS, BOARS, AND BULLS.

LEWISHAM

ENFIELD

TOWER HAMLETS

KENSINGTON & CHELSEA

WATCH OUT! SEA MONSTERS ABOUT!

NATIONAL MARITIME MUSEUM, GREENWICH

If you look at ocean maps made before the 1800s, you might think the seas were swarming with fearsome monsters. Greenwich's National Maritime Museum is home to many of these monster-infested maps, showing oversized octopuses, sea serpents, mermaids, and giant fish with wolflike fangs.

SECRETS REVEALED!

Become a city spy and tiptoe around some of London's hidden surprises and top-secret locations.

TOP SECRET

PADDINGTON BASIN

NOW YOU SEE IT...

THE ROLLING BRIDGE, PADDINGTON BASIN

On most days this is a regular-looking bridge – a steel and wooden footbridge that is 39 feet (12 m) long, to be precise. But at noon each Friday, it reveals its crazy secret! It rolls up into an octagon shape, activated by hydraulic pistons, allowing boats to pass. British designer Thomas Heatherwick came up with the concept, and it was completed in 2004.

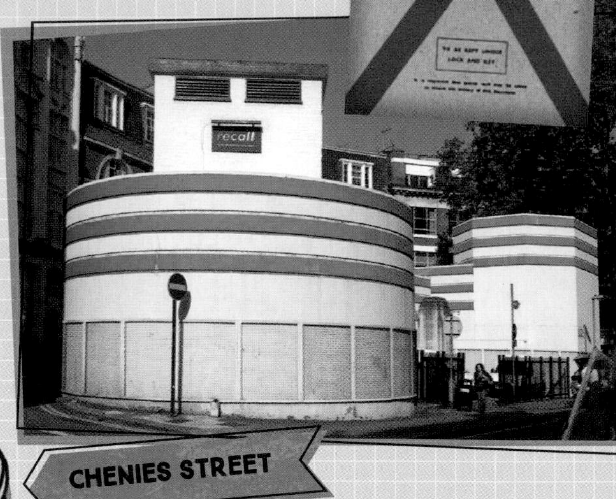

CHENIES STREET

WEIRD WAR BASE

EISENHOWER'S AIR-RAID SHELTER, CHENIES STREET

A red-and-white-striped pillbox on Chenies Street, near Goodge Street Station, is thought to have been the location for an important secret meeting. It is the entrance to a World War II air-raid shelter down below, once equipped with bunk beds, kitchens, and medical facilities. The secret meeting was between US General Dwight Eisenhower and other top leaders when planning D-day – the Allied troops' invasion of Europe that led to the end of the war.

THAMES HOUSE

SPY CENTRAL

THAMES HOUSE AND VAUXHALL CROSS

MI5 is the British intelligence agency that works to protect national security against terrorism and espionage. MI6 is the agency responsible for dealing with overseas threats – and forever associated with fictional spy James Bond. MI5's headquarters, designed by architect Terry Farrell, is at Thames House, and MI6 stares at it suspiciously from across the water at Vauxhall Cross.

THE MI6 BUILDING IS BLOWN UP IN THE JAMES BOND MOVIE *SKYFALL*.

PHONES FROM BONES

ST. PANCRAS OLD CHURCH

There's a surprising secret behind London's iconic red phone booths. Sir Giles Gilbert Scott, who first designed the booths in 1924, was inspired by the mausoleum (tomb) of architect Sir John Soane and his family in a churchyard in St. Pancras. Scott used the tomb shape as a model for his iron phone booths, which were painted red to make them easy to spot.

SECRET SNIFF

ADMIRALTY ARCH

In 1997, artist Rick Buckley made plaster of Paris models of his nose and used them to create an artistic installation found on buildings in London. Initially around 35 noses were made, but now only 9 survive, including one at Admiralty Arch. There's also an ear on a wall in Floral Street, Covent Garden, put there by artist Tim Fishlock.

search: SECRET SOCIETIES

WHO K-NOSE?

It is thought that artist Rick Buckley created the *London Noses* as a statement against the nosy CCTV cameras dotted all over the city, but nobody "k-nose" for sure.

NOT-SO-SECRET SOCIETIES

FREEMASONS' HALL, HOLBORN

(AND OTHER PLACES WE DON'T KNOW ABOUT)

London has been a hotbed of secret societies throughout history. The Freemasons are probably the most famous, though they're no longer secret and visitors can tour their headquarters in Holborn. A much sillier example from history was the Calves' Head Club, which was devoted to making fun of the beheaded King Charles I. Members would meet in different houses on January 30 each year to celebrate the anniversary of the king's execution, and as a sick joke, they feasted on a roasted calf's head. They had to disband in 1734 when an angry mob put a stop to their not-so-secret dinner shenanigans.

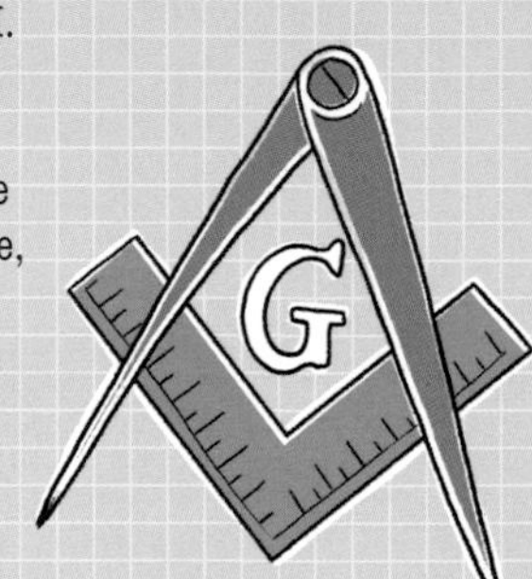

THE ONCE-SECRET SYMBOL OF THE FREEMASONS!

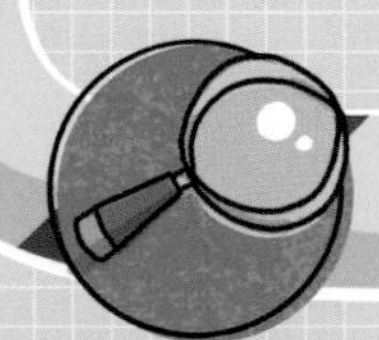

HOLBORN

ALIEN HIDEOUTS

CENTRAL STREET
AND OTHER LOCATIONS

Mysterious French street artist "Invader" has hidden dozens of tiled mosaics depicting Space Invaders all around London. The mosaic alien visitors have been spotted on Central Street, Old Brewer's Yard, and other locations in central, southwest, and east London. The same artist tiled a battle between Darth Vader and Luke Skywalker on the side of a building in Shoreditch, and has also "invaded" 65 other cities around the world, leaving his space invader art.

CENTRAL STREET

RING OF BLOOD

ROMAN AMPHITHEATRE, GUILDHALL

For centuries, no one knew the murderous secret lurking beneath London's Guildhall. Then, in 1988, some ruins were uncovered. The ancient walls turned out to be 2,000 years old and part of a Roman amphitheater. Here, gladiators fought to the death, and armed battles between man and beast took place – all unfolding in front of a roaring crowd of thousands. Today visitors can step into the remains of the ancient gladiator ring and experience sights and sounds re-created by an exhibition.

GUILDHALL

LET'S SEE THE SHOW!

London's always buzzing with entertainment. On this trail we've laid out plays, movies, a flower show, a mega-carnival, and some street entertainers for you. Oh, and by the way, there's a ghostly hand and hovering head, too!

THE BIG BLOOM

CHELSEA FLOWER SHOW, ROYAL HOSPITAL

Every spring, thousands of flowers take over the grounds of the Royal Hospital, Chelsea. Welcome to the Chelsea Flower Show, the gardener's equivalent of the Olympics. Garden designers and plant growers compete for medals, with ever more fantastical designs and incredible blooms. For a while, garden gnomes were banned from the show and it became a challenge for people to smuggle them in. They were allowed back in 2013.

2x SOCCER FIELDS
THE SIZE OF THE GREAT PAVILION, THE BIGGEST FLOWER MARQUEE

157,000
VISITORS EACH YEAR

50,000
CUPS OF TEA AND COFFEE DRUNK

PARTY!

NOTTING HILL CARNIVAL

August's annual Notting Hill Carnival is London's biggest street party. It's famous for its steel-drum parades and the brightly colored costumes of performers dancing through the streets. More than a million carnival revelers join in the party over a long weekend.

NOTTING HILL

Over **22 MILLION** people go to London shows each year.

That brings in around **US$1,060 MILLION** a year. Now that's a star performance!

There are about **240 THEATER SPACES** around town, with more than **110,000 SEATS** between them.

STAR STAGES

THEATRELAND

AND OTHER LOCATIONS

They say that more people go to the theater in London than anywhere else in the world, with the biggest productions taking place in Theatreland, the nickname for an area in the West End of London, where there are lots of theaters. Check out the super stats on the left. Curtains up, please!

THEATRELAND

FINAL NIGHT FIGHT

COLISEUM, ST. MARTIN'S LANE

The 2,359-seat Coliseum is the capital's biggest theater. One of the strangest (and funniest) nights happened here in 1933, and the story made all the newspapers. On the final night of the play *Casanova*, two actors who hated each other got into a fight as the cast took their final bows. Every time the curtain came down after each encore, the men started fighting again. "I had to hold them apart while the curtain went up and down about seven times," said one of the actresses.

ST. MARTIN'S THEATRE

MOUSE MURDER

THE MOUSETRAP, ST. MARTIN'S THEATRE, WEST STREET

The world's longest-running play, *The Mousetrap*, first opened in 1952, and it's still going strong more than 60 years later after more than 25,000 performances. It's a murder mystery by Agatha Christie. After the show, the audience is asked never to reveal the murderer, so we won't either!

search: WEST END SHOW RECORDS

OVER 12,000 PERFORMANCES	**Les Misérables**	Opened October 8, 1985
OVER 12,000 PERFORMANCES	**The Phantom of the Opera**	Opened October 9, 1986
OVER 10,000 PERFORMANCES	**The Woman in Black**	Opened January 15, 1989

THEATRE ROYAL DRURY LANE

SPOOKIEST STAGE

THEATRE ROYAL DRURY LANE, CATHERINE STREET

The Theatre Royal Drury Lane is reputed to be London's most haunted theater, with several ghosts said to be hanging around long after their final curtain call. There's the "Man in Grey," who sits in the audience in a wig and cloak from the 1700s. Then there's the disembodied head of clown Joseph Grimaldi, occasionally spotted hovering in one of the theater boxes, and there's even a "helping hand" ghost who apparently pushes actors into better positions on stage and pats them on the back if they do well.

SOUTH BANK

SHOW IN THE STREET

SOUTH BANK

London bustles with lively street entertainers, but the South Bank is home to a cast of performers who do absolutely nothing. They're living statues, and they earn money by standing stock-still to impress passers-by enough that they'll throw some coins. It might sound like an easy way to make a living, but standing immobile for hours on end is really hard. The top tip from a London living statue? Always eat before you start. You don't want to faint or your tummy to rumble!

VARIOUS LOCATIONS

SOAPY STARS

HOT TUB CINEMA, VARIOUS LOCATIONS

London is Britain's movie theater center, and the stars often arrive via the red carpet for big-name premieres. The biggest, plushest movie theaters are around Leicester Square, but there's a funny new London trend for seeing movies a different way – while sitting in a bubbly hot tub! Hot-tub movie fans can relax among the bubbles while they see the show.

SHAKESPEARE'S STAGE

THE GLOBE

THE GLOBE, SOUTHWARK

Britain's most famous playwright, William Shakespeare, lived and worked in London roughly 400 years ago, in Tudor times. One of the theaters where his plays were performed was the Globe, which stood on the southern bank of the Thames. Today there's a modern reconstruction close to the original site, based on drawings and descriptions from history.

BOOZY BOAT TRIP

In Shakespeare's day, theaters were banned in the stuffy city of London, so people paid a penny to travel over the river by boat to Southwark. It was the party zone of Tudor London, where playgoers could also get drunk in taverns and gamble on cockfights or bear-baiting.

LADS AS LADIES

Women weren't allowed on stage in Shakespeare's time, so the female parts were played by boys. There was stiff competition among boy actors for the best parts, but once they grew and their voices changed, there was no guarantee they could continue.

THE CHEAP SEATS

The cheapest tickets at the Globe were for the "yard" in front of the stage, where crowds stood watching the play, heckling and even throwing things. We know they ate hazelnuts and oranges as they watched, and they probably drank ale, too. They would have got wet if it rained.

STOP!

In Tudor times, plays could only be performed if the actors were given permission by royal officials. If they thought the play was too controversial, they wouldn't allow it. Plays were banned in London in the 1640s for being disgraceful and a bad influence. The theaters were closed for a while but reopened again 20 years later, when women were finally allowed to perform for the first time.

FIRE!

In 1613, the Globe Theatre went up in flames during a performance of Shakespeare's *Henry VIII.* A cannon used as a prop misfired, setting fire to the roof. According to reports at the time, nobody was hurt except a man who had to put out the flames on his burning breeches with a bottle of ale.

EACH PILLAR ON THE STAGE IS ONE OAK TREE

OVER 1,000

THE NUMBER OF TREES USED TO BUILD THE NEW GLOBE

FAKE FIGHTING

THERE WERE NO BIG PIECES OF SCENERY, BUT THE ACTORS USED PROPS, INCLUDING REAL SWORDS THAT SOMETIMES CAUSED NASTY ACCIDENTS ON STAGE. IN A STAGE FIGHT AN ACTOR MIGHT WEAR A SHEEP'S BLADDER FILLED WITH ANIMAL BLOOD UNDER HIS COSTUME, READY TO BURST AND CREATE THE ILLUSION OF A DEADLY WOUND.

WEAR LONDON

London is one of the world's fashion hubs and it's home to some world-famous outfits and uniforms, too. Tread the style trail to find out who's wearing what... and where.

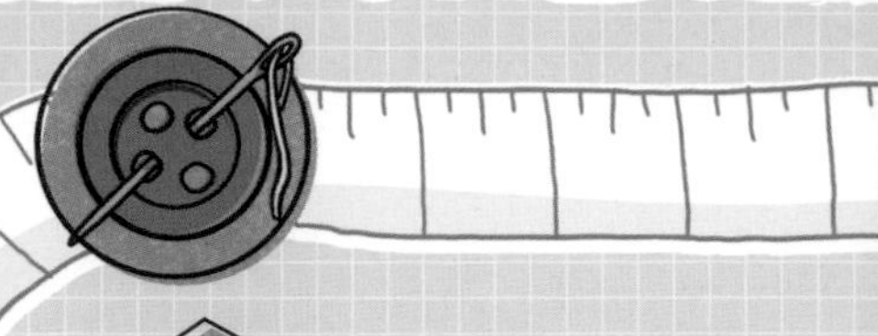

BUCKINGHAM PALACE & ST. JAMES'S PALACE

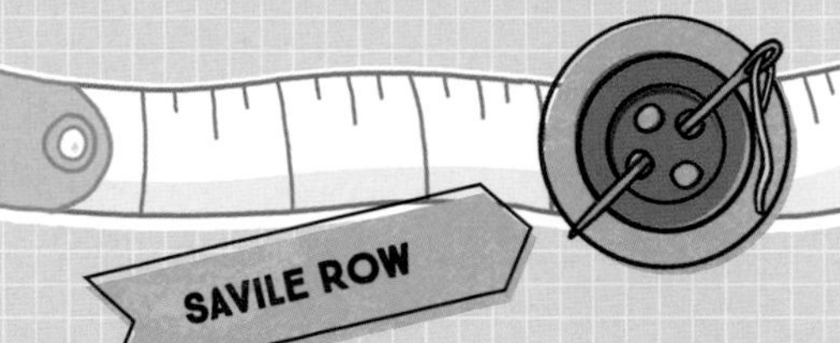

SAVILE ROW

SUITS YOU

SAVILE ROW

This Mayfair street is world famous for bespoke (handmade) men's suits. It's said that the dinner jacket (called a tuxedo) was invented here. That's the jacket James Bond wears with a bow tie when he goes to parties. There have been many famous Savile Row clients through history. Horatio Nelson, the hero on top of the column in Trafalgar Square, was wearing a Savile Row–made uniform when he was killed at the Battle of Trafalgar.

FURRY HEAD, DRESSED IN RED

BUCKINGHAM PALACE & ST. JAMES'S PALACE

The Queen's Guard stands on duty at Buckingham Palace and St. James's Palace. The guards sport red tunics and bearskin hats in summer and greatcoats in winter. Their uniforms come from a time when soldiers fought on foot. The tall bearskin caps were probably devised to make them look taller in battle, and their red tunics made it harder for the enemy to count them on the battlefield (they tend to blur into each other in a crowd).

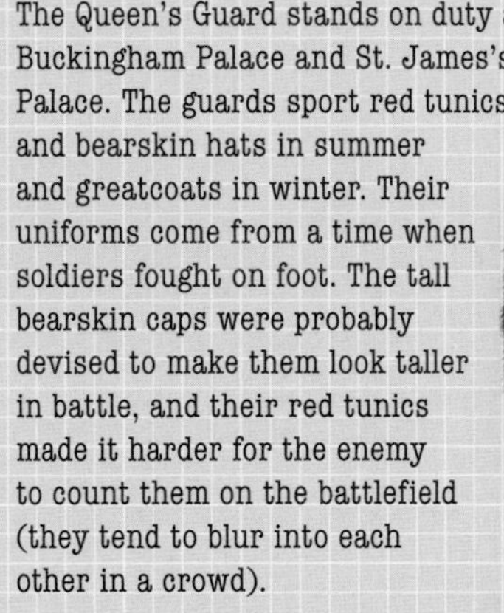

WHEN THE QUEEN IS AT THE PALACE, THERE ARE USUALLY FOUR GUARDS OUT FRONT. WHEN SHE'S AWAY, THERE ARE TWO.

CAMDEN TOWN

PUNK PLACE

CAMDEN TOWN

London is famous for jump-starting the 1970s–early 1980s punk era. The punk bands not only had their own music style, they had their own look, too. They enjoyed shocking people with their brightly dyed, gravity-defying Mohawk hairstyles and their many safety pins, worn on clothes or as body piercings. A few punks still wander around Camden Town, where they get photographed by tourists. Now they're not at the forefront of fashion – they're wearing historical costumes!

SOHO AND COVENT GARDEN

STYLE CITY

LONDON FASHION WEEK, SOHO & COVENT GARDEN

Each February and September, London Fashion Week showcases the best designers, flashy new clothing, and cutting-edge trends in a series of fashion shows and events. Think clothes are boring? Here they aren't! There are always some crazy-looking outfits on show. Models have been seen wearing giant lampshades, green face paint, or even mouse ears.

ROYAL ROBES

EDE & RAVENSCROFT, CHANCERY LANE

Tailors Ede & Ravenscroft have been the royal robe makers for hundreds of years. They made the robe Queen Elizabeth II wore for her 1953 coronation. It had a train 21 feet (6.4 m) long, in handmade crimson silk velvet, trimmed with Canadian ermine fur, lined with pure silk, and embroidered with thread made of real gold. Six maids-of-honor helped carry the heavy train, with smelling salts hidden in their gloves in case they felt faint during the ceremony!

BRIGHT FOR A BANK

BANK OF ENGLAND

Well-dressed doormen greet people at London's top hotels around town, but the gatekeepers at the Bank of England take the prize for the gaudiest getup. Nobody could miss them at the entrance to Britain's top bank because they sport pink jackets, red vests, and top hats with gold trim.

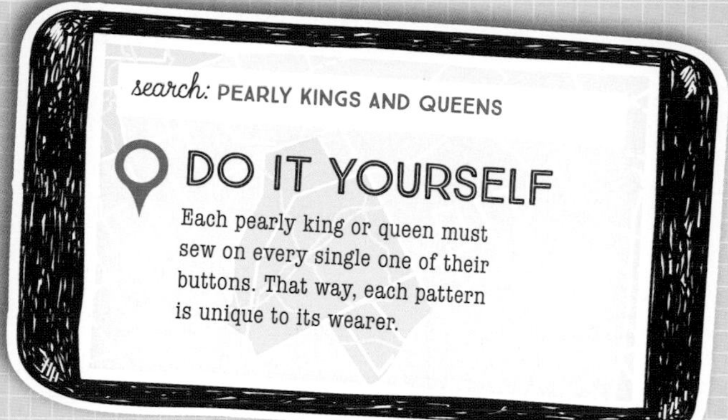

search: PEARLY KINGS AND QUEENS

DO IT YOURSELF

Each pearly king or queen must sew on every single one of their buttons. That way, each pattern is unique to its wearer.

CHARITY KINGS AND QUEENS

EAST END

Pearly kings and queens cover their clothes in shiny buttons and make appearances around London raising money for charity. The tradition comes from the costermongers – the street traders of London who began decorating their clothes in the 1800s to make themselves stand out. Street cleaner and rat catcher Henry Croft went one better and decorated his whole outfit with buttons, becoming the very first pearly king.

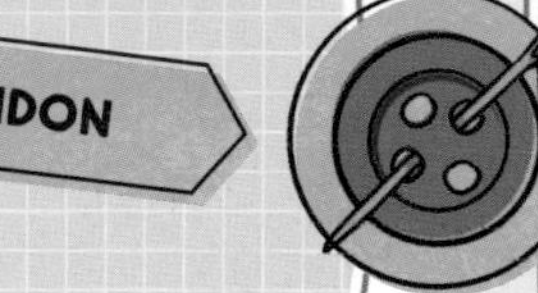

MUSEUM OF LONDON

ANCIENT UNDIES

MUSEUM OF LONDON

Thought bikinis were a modern invention? Wrong! A pair of leather bikini briefs dating from ancient Roman times were found down an old well in Queen Street. They look like a modern beach bikini with ties at the sides. It's thought that they were probably part of an outfit worn by acrobatic dancers. Beachwear wouldn't really make sense in London, after all.

RIGHT ROYAL ROUTE

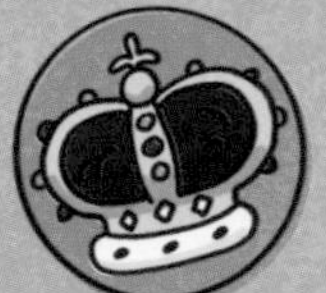

Britain has had kings and queens for over 1,000 years, and London is now the glittering center of the royal kingdom. Imagine if you ruled! London's grandest palaces would be yours. This trail is designed to provide you with some royal insider information, just in case you ever do get to sit on the British throne (you never know). This way, your majesty...

HYDE PARK

ROYAL SPOOK STORIES

HAMPTON COURT PALACE

Hampton Court Palace is said to be one of the most haunted royal residences. The screams of Catherine Howard, executed by her Tudor husband Henry VIII, are rumored to echo through the walls. Another Hampton phantom with royal connections is the "Grey Lady," thought to be Elizabeth I's nursemaid, Sybil Penn, who sits spinning at her wheel. The jury is out on the identity of Hampton's "Skeletor," however. This creepy cloaked cadaver was spotted on CCTV footage in 2003, but is probably just a fake phantom!

A DIP FOR DIANA

DIANA MEMORIAL FOUNTAIN, HYDE PARK

This lovely watery wonder was built to honor Diana, Princess of Wales, who tragically died in a car crash in 1997. It's made from 545 pieces of Cornish granite that fit together like a jigsaw. The water flows in two directions and swirls into a tranquil pond at the bottom. Visitors can wander over the bridges or dip their toes in for a paddle.

EAT LIKE ROYALTY

BUCKINGHAM PALACE BANQUET

Buckingham Palace is the venue for royal banquets when important guests visit. It takes three days to lay the enormous banqueting table with thousands of pieces of cutlery and glasses (every guest has six glasses for the different wines), along with carefully folded napkins. Each guest gets a space of 16.5 inches (42 cm) for their place setting, and it's all carefully measured. During the mega-dinners, there are so many courses that the serving staff uses a traffic light system behind the scenes to make sure they're all coordinated.

THE SPEEDIEST ROYAL EATER EVER WAS QUEEN VICTORIA, WHO COULD GET THROUGH 7 BANQUET COURSES IN 30 MINUTES. AS SOON AS SHE HAD FINISHED, EVERYBODY'S PLATES WERE CLEARED AWAY, SO HER PANICKY GUESTS HAD TO TRY TO KEEP UP WITH HER GREEDY GOBBLING!

GET YOUR CROWN HERE

WESTMINSTER ABBEY

It doesn't get more royal than this. Westminster Abbey has been the site of the coronation of every British monarch since William the Conqueror was crowned in 1066. A range of royal rear ends have sat on the Coronation Chair in the abbey, which is a UNESCO World Heritage site. Prince William married Kate Middleton here in 2011.

UK'S TOP CHAIR

The wooden Coronation Chair was made on the orders of Edward I in 1300. He had a space put underneath to house the Stone of Scone – the sacred stone of Scotland that Scottish kings sat on when they got crowned. Now the space is empty and the Stone of Scone is in Edinburgh Castle, but it will be brought back for coronations in the future.

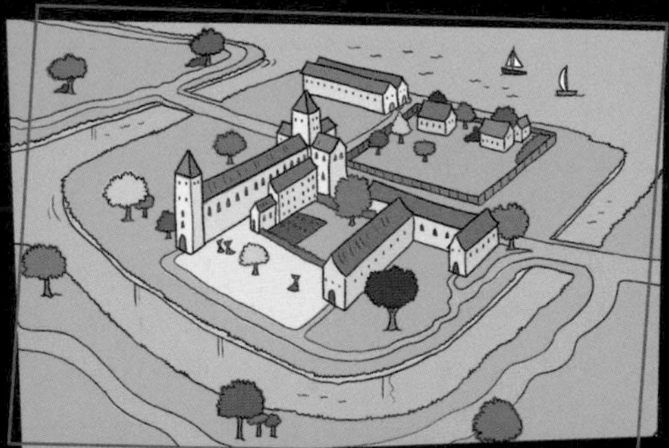

MADE FOR MONKS

When the abbey was first built nearly 1,000 years ago, it was on an island. Over time, the land has been drained so it's not an island any more. For centuries, monks lived here, and the abbey had its own farm and gardens. There's still a peaceful herb garden, where the monks once grew the plants they needed for food and to make medicine.

SPACE FOR THE STONE OF SCONE

ROYAL RESTING PLACE

Among the 450 tombs and monuments at Westminster Abbey are monarchs' graves, including those of Tudor rulers Henry VIII, Mary, and Elizabeth I (right). It's also the final resting place of notable non-royalty, including scientist Charles Darwin and authors Geoffrey Chaucer and Charles Dickens.

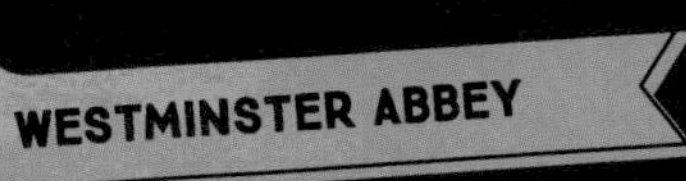

GRAFFITI

The Coronation Chair has lots of graffiti carved on it by Westminster schoolboys in the 1700s and 1800s. One line says: P. Abbott slept in this chair 5:6 July 1800.

CHRISTMAS CRISIS

WILLIAM THE CONQUERER, CROWNED AT THE ABBEY ON CHRISTMAS DAY, 1066, HAD A CORONATION TO REMEMBER. HE CAME FROM NORMANDY IN NORTHERN FRANCE AND HAD INVADED ENGLAND, FORCING LONDON TO ACCEPT HIM AS RULER. AT THE CEREMONY, THE ENGLISH NOBLES WERE ASKED TO ACCEPT HIM AS KING AND THEY SHOUTED THEIR AGREEMENT – WHICH IS TRADITIONAL. BUT THE FRENCH GUARDS OUTSIDE DIDN'T KNOW THAT. THEY THOUGHT THERE WAS TROUBLE, AND STARTED SETTING FIRE TO BUILDINGS! THE TERRIFIED CORONATION GUESTS RUSHED OUT, LEAVING THE TREMBLING KING WITH JUST A FEW PRIESTS TO FINISH THE CERLMONY.

SPLINTERED BUT SURVIVED

The Coronation Chair only just survived the 1900s. In 1914, suffragettes fighting for women's rights put a small bomb under the chair, and when it exploded, it blew a piece off. In 1950, Scottish students stole the Stone of Scone from under it, damaging the chair and accidentally dropping the stone, breaking it in half.

GREAT MAN ON MONEY

KING ALFRED PENNY, BRITISH MUSEUM

It's hard to get "the Great" added to your name, but Anglo-Saxon King Alfred the Great (849–899) managed it by defending the southern part of Britain from the Vikings. Throughout the 890s, he found ingenious ways to stop the Danish Vikings from sailing up the Thames, but the local Anglo-Saxons had a tough time before Alfred turned up. In 842, a Viking army laid waste to the thatched huts of Lundenwic (London's name at the time) in a terrible attack called the "Great Slaughter," which says it all.

BRITISH MUSEUM

IN THE BRITISH MUSEUM THERE'S A RARE ANGLO-SAXON SILVER PENNY MARKED "LONDONIA," SHOWING A PICTURE OF KING ALFRED.

MASSIVE MUMMY BOX

SIR JOHN SOANE'S MUSEUM, LINCOLN'S INN FIELDS

In 1824, collector Sir John Soane managed to buy the sarcophagus (stone coffin) of ancient Egyptian royalty Seti I, and he had a three-day party around it to celebrate. Seti's mummy lives in Cairo, but his sarcophagus is on show in Soane's London-based museum. Incredibly, it was carved around 3,000 years ago from one massive piece of alabaster. It's decorated with carvings, including one of the fun-sounding Egyptian goddess Nut. Seti was one of ancient Egypt's most powerful rulers, and his tomb is the biggest found so far in Egypt's Valley of the Kings.

BAD NEWS BY BELL

ST. PAUL'S CATHEDRAL

Royal events aplenty, including weddings and thanksgiving services, have taken place in St. Paul's, the cathedral of the City of London. It has 12 bells, providing one of the biggest bell rings in the world, and it takes several years for new bell-ringers to learn how to work them. The biggest bells are Great Paul, weighing more than a fully grown male elephant, and Great Tom, weighing about as much as a female elephant. It's Great Tom that tolls out the bad news across town if a member of the royal family dies.

TOP CHOP SPOT

CHAPEL ROYAL, TOWER OF LONDON

There was once a time when anyone important who upset a monarch risked having their head cut off here, on Tower Green outside the Chapel Royal. It was considered a five-star execution spot. Most prisoners had their heads lopped off in front of a baying crowd on Tower Hill, but this private site was reserved for the most important aristocratic prisoners. Three English queens were beheaded here: Anne Boleyn (1536), Catherine Howard (1542), and Lady Jane Grey (1554). There is now a memorial, in the shape of a glass cushion, on the exact spot where the execution block once stood.

TOWER OF LONDON

WATERY LONDON

Anchors away! Set sail along this trail for a peek at all things wavy and watery. No walking needed this time. Just keep paddling!

RIVER THAMES

THE RIVER'S THE REASON

RIVER THAMES

England's longest river runs through London and it was probably the reason why people settled here in the first place, around 750,000 years ago, when it was a marshy wilderness. The first Londoners built their prehistoric huts where they could fish and perhaps get across the river. They built wooden walkways over the marshes, too. The remains of one such walkway was discovered in Greenwich, dating back 6,000 years. That's more than 500 years older than Stonehenge!

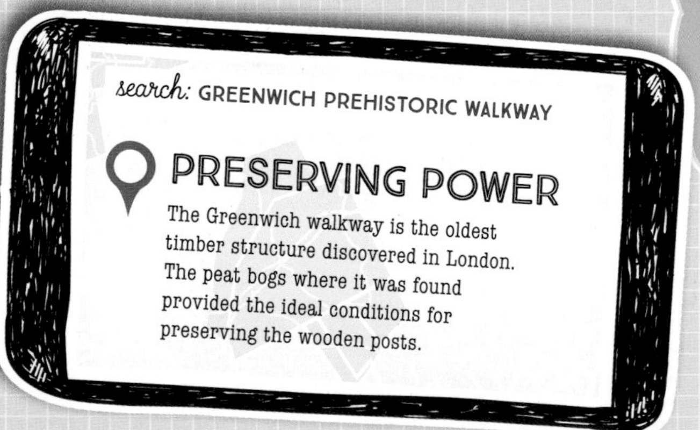

search: GREENWICH PREHISTORIC WALKWAY

PRESERVING POWER

The Greenwich walkway is the oldest timber structure discovered in London. The peat bogs where it was found provided the ideal conditions for preserving the wooden posts.

PIRATES AHOY!

PIRATE CASTLE, CAMDEN LOCK

Aharrr! There's a pirate castle in the heart of London, make no mistake, Cap'n! It's a sailing club and theater for children, and it all began in 1966 when kindly local Lord St. Davids, who lived by the river, began collecting and repairing old boats for local children to use. He founded the club for mini-pirates to learn to sail on the canal, and in return they nicknamed him Peg-leg. His cool canal-based charity continues today in its mock canal-side castle.

CAMDEN LOCK

DEATH TURNED OFF

CHOLERA WATER PUMP, BROADWICK STREET

It's a replica of the original, but the black pump on Broadwick Street is a memorial to how a smart doctor called John Snow stopped a deadly cholera epidemic raging through London – by simply turning off a tap. In the 1854 Broad Street cholera epidemic, 616 local people died in just a few days. Then John Snow linked the outbreak to dirty water. He took the handle off the street's water pump and the outbreak ground to a halt. It was a major breakthrough in discovering that cholera was spread by contaminated water, not by air as had been thought.

THE BRITISH MUSEUM

REALM OF THE RIVER GODS

THE BRITISH MUSEUM

Way back in the river mists of time, people thought that the Thames was a place where magic spirits lived, and they threw offerings into the water. Around 2,300 years ago, a beautiful and finely made bronze shield was thrown in near what is now the site of Battersea Bridge. The shield is decorated with swirls and polished red glass, and might have been specially made for a mysterious throwing-in ceremony. Perhaps the local tribe wanted the river gods to help them in some way. The shield is now on display at the British Museum.

TOTTENHAM COURT ROAD

THE BIG BEER FLOOD

TOTTENHAM COURT ROAD

London has occasionally had floods, but in 1814 there was an unusually sticky disaster. About 320,000 gallons (1,210,000 liters) of beer flooded out of the Meux and Company brewery, when giant vats of the brew burst and toppled. The wave was 15 feet (4.6 m) high, and went down Tottenham Court Road, destroying two houses and killing seven people. The Dominion Theatre is now on the site of the old brewery, but people in the local pub still have a memorial flood drink every year.

SWAYING SPAN

MILLENNIUM BRIDGE

London's Millenium Bridge opened in 2000, but it was soon closed when it began to sway dangerously, as pedestrians tried to walk across. It turned out their footsteps were making it swing. The bridge cost US$27 million to build, and another US$7.6 million to repair. The bridge had a starring role in Harry Potter, too. In the *Harry Potter and the Half-Blood Prince* movie, the bridge was destroyed by the Death Eaters. Perhaps they were fed up with the wobble!

MONEY IN MUD

MUSEUM OF LONDON DOCKLANDS

Muddying your hands on the riverbank might sound like good fun, but imagine having to do it to stay alive. "Mudlarks" were poor Victorian children who scrabbled around on the banks of the Thames looking for anything of value to sell. They might find scraps of wood, tin, or, if they were really lucky, a fancy brooch. But most of the time it was filthy, dangerous work. Dead rats and poop were more likely finds – along with deadly cholera germs. There's a Mudlarks Gallery at the Museum of London Docklands, commemorating the mud-sifting children of the river.

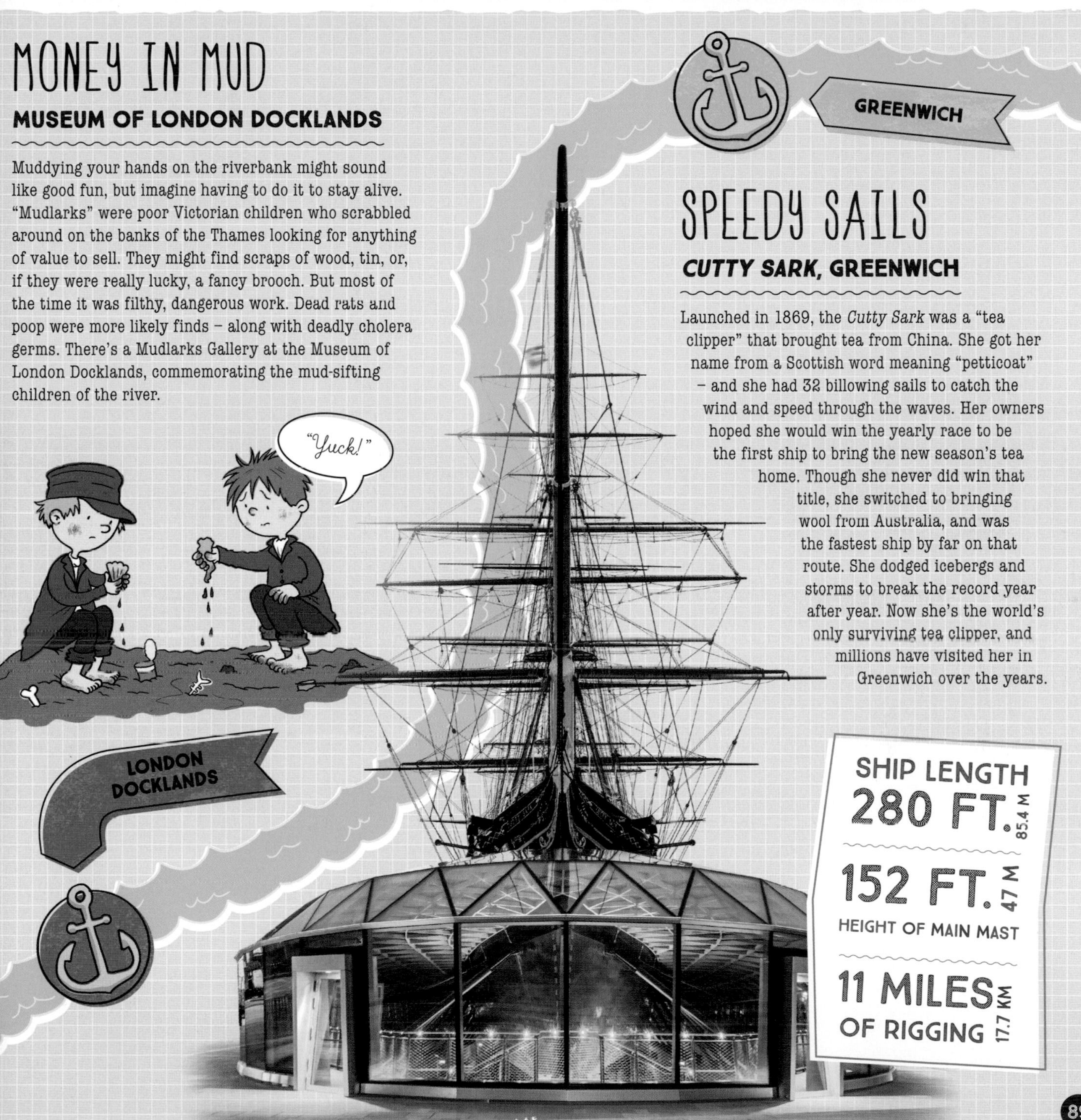

SPEEDY SAILS

CUTTY SARK, GREENWICH

Launched in 1869, the *Cutty Sark* was a "tea clipper" that brought tea from China. She got her name from a Scottish word meaning "petticoat" – and she had 32 billowing sails to catch the wind and speed through the waves. Her owners hoped she would win the yearly race to be the first ship to bring the new season's tea home. Though she never did win that title, she switched to bringing wool from Australia, and was the fastest ship by far on that route. She dodged icebergs and storms to break the record year after year. Now she's the world's only surviving tea clipper, and millions have visited her in Greenwich over the years.

SHIP LENGTH
280 FT. 85.4 M

152 FT. 47 M
HEIGHT OF MAIN MAST

11 MILES 17.7 KM
OF RIGGING

SPORTY LONDON

London may be a built-up city, but it's got plenty of space for sports. Here are some unusually active facts that make this trail a winner!

500,000 SPECTATORS OVER TWO WEEKS

39,000 MAXIMUM EACH DAY

STAR SERVES

ALL ENGLAND CLUB, WIMBLEDON

One of the top tennis competitions on the planet is played right here in the leafy London suburb of Wimbledon. Nowadays it's watched by around 1.2 billion TV viewers, but the event began way back in 1877, long before TV, making it the world's oldest tennis tournament.

OLD-SCHOOL TENNIS

It wasn't until 1930 that the first player turned up at Wimbledon wearing shorts. Up until then the players wore long pants.

WIMBLEDON

STRAWBERRY FIELDS

Anyone watching Wimbledon on site will be tempted to tuck into the traditional courtside snack of strawberries and cream. It's estimated that around 142,000 strawberries are gobbled down by Wimbledon spectators during the tournament, topped with 1,540 gallons (7,000 liters) of cream.

NEW BALLS, PLEASE!

An estimated 54,250 tennis balls are used during the two-week tournament, and each one is pre-tested to make sure it has the right weight, bounce, and compression (squeezability). Around 700 schoolchildren apply for the position of ball girl and ball boy. Only 200 successfully complete the training course and help out at the matches.

HAWKEYE FOR REAL

HAWKEYE IS THE NICKNAME GIVEN TO THE ELECTRONIC MACHINE THAT CHECKS IF THE TENNIS BALLS ARE IN OR OUT DURING MATCHES, BUT THERE'S A REAL HAWKEYE WORKING AT WIMBLEDON, TOO. EVERY MORNING BEFORE THE CLUB OPENS, A TRAINED HAWK IS SET FREE TO FLY AROUND FOR AN HOUR AND SCARE OFF THE PESKY PIGEONS WHO OTHERWISE MIGHT DISRUPT PLAY OR PERHAPS EVEN POOP ON THE PLAYERS.

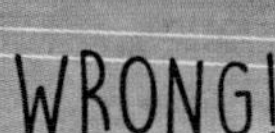

WRONG!

The very first Wimbledon champion, Spencer Gore, said that he doubted the game would ever catch on. Perhaps he got the idea that it wouldn't be a big deal because there were only 22 players taking part that year. His final was atched by 200 people, who each payed a shilling (about 8 cents) to see it.

FROM CABBAGES TO CUPS

TWICKENHAM STADIUM

Twickenham is the home of the English Rugby Union. It can hold 82,000 people, making it the world's largest dedicated rugby union stadium. It's got a strange history for a sports stadium, though. The first game was played here in 1909, but before that, it was a cabbage patch! During World War I, it was used to graze horses, and in World War II, it was set up as a decontamination center in the event of a chemical attack.

WORLD-RECORD WEMBLEY

WEMBLEY STADIUM

Europe's second-largest stadium has a massive 90,000-spectator capacity. It hosts the England soccer team's home games and FA Cup final games. The stadium space is the equivalent of 25,000 double-decker buses, and its restrooms are record-breakers. There are 2,618 restrooms – more than any other venue in the world.

SHIVERY DIPS

HAMPSTEAD HEATH

Warning signs about algae and freezing temperatures don't deter the wild swimmers of North London. On Hampstead Heath there's a Ladies' Pond, a Men's Pond, and a pond for everyone. The Ladies' and Men's Ponds are unique in the UK. They are the only outdoor swimming spots with lifeguards that open to the public every single day of the year. Yes... even in midwinter hardy Hampstead swimmers take icy dips here.

search: LONDON SOCCER FACTS

OLDEST CLUB

FULHAM Founded 1879

MOST SUCCESSFUL

ARSENAL
12x FA Cups
13x Football League championships

BRAINY BOXING

HAZELVILLE ROAD, ISLINGTON

Londoners who like to think and throw punches are catered for with chess-boxing. Brain meets brawn in this new sport, where fast-paced rounds of chess are punctuated by rounds of fisticuffs. You can either win by a knockout – or a less painful checkmate!

GO GIRLZ!

CRYSTAL PALACE NATIONAL SPORTS CENTRE

High-speed skate chases are all the rage in London. A roller derby involves two teams of five going around a track on skates. In a series of "jams," a "jammer" on each team attempts to score points by lapping members of the other team. It's a contact sport, so things can get ugly when teams try to hamper the opposing team's jammer. The London Roller Girls can be credited with cementing the craze in the British capital, as the oldest established all-female roller derby league. The roller derby teams and the audience like to dress punk style, with candy stripe socks and skull and crossbones T-shirts often on show.

CRYSTAL PALACE

THE ASHES URN IS SACRED TO CRICKET FANS AND IS KEPT AT LORDS, HOME OF CRICKET.

LORD'S CRICKET GROUND

URN-ING THE ASHES

LORD'S CRICKET GROUND

When the England cricket team first lost on home soil to Australia in 1882, a newspaper announced the death of English cricket: "The body will be cremated and the ashes taken to Australia." When the England team next went to Australia, they were given a tiny urn representing "the Ashes," and the two teams still play a hotly contested series of games for the Ashes to this day.

300 YEARS OF ROWING

LONDON BRIDGE

Every summer one of the world's oldest sporting contests takes place on the Thames, when six rowers race for the honor of winning the "Doggett's Coat and Badge" – a scarlet uniform with a huge silver medallion the size of a dinner plate on the sleeve. Young watermen who have qualified to work on the river can take part, rowing between London Bridge and Chelsea.

THE BIG YEAR

QUEEN ELIZABETH OLYMPIC PARK

LONDON BRIDGE

London is the only city in the world to host the Olympics three times – in 1908, 1948, and 2012. Nine hundred million people worldwide tuned in to the 2012 opening ceremony at the Olympic Park, and among the many Olympic records broken, the most celebrated was sprinter Usain Bolt's 9.63-second 100-meter marvel. Things were different in the first two London Olympics. The 1908 competition included tug-of-war, powerboat racing, and polo. The 1948 event had an artistic competition as well as a sporting one, and medals were given out for painting, sculpture, and architecture.

PLEASED TO MEET YOU

Step this way to meet a few of the people and animals who have statues around town. Some of them really did live in London, and some come from the imagination. Either way, they've got great stories to tell.

ALBERT EMBANKMENT

SECRET AGENTS' STATUE

SOE MEMORIAL, ALBERT EMBANKMENT

World War II secret agents have their own commemorative statue. The agents remembered here worked for a secret government organization called the Special Operations Executive and undertook daring undercover missions. On top of the plinth is a statue of Violetta Szabo, a secret agent who worked in France but was captured during a mission and executed. After her death, she was awarded the highest possible bravery medals by both Britain and France.

PADDINGTON BEAR BOOKS HAVE SOLD MORE THAN 300 MILLION COPIES WORLDWIDE.

PADDINGTON BEAR STATUE

PADDINGTON STATION

Paddington, the friendly bear from Peru who is never far from his favorite marmalade sandwiches, has starred in 70 stories since he was introduced in 1958 by author Michael Bond. Bond was inspired by a little bear he bought on Christmas Eve in 1956. He named his character after Paddington Station, near his home, and there's a bronze statue of the bear in the station to remind us of where he was found.

PADDINGTON STATION

WESTMINSTER BRIDGE

STATUE WITH ATTITUDE

BOUDICCA STATUE, WESTMINSTER BRIDGE

Next to Westminster Bridge you'll find one of Britain's great women leaders – Boudicca, queen of the Celtic Iceni tribe. She's shown riding a chariot, as she would have done when she attacked Roman Londinium in 61 BC. Her warriors killed hundreds and burned the town to the ground in revenge for Roman ill treatment of her tribe. Archaeologists have found a layer of charred soil deep under London, evidence of her ferocious and fiery attack on the town.

ANIMAL HEROES

ANIMALS IN WAR MEMORIAL PARK LANE

This monument celebrates all the brave beasts that have been used in war, especially the 60 or so creatures awarded the top animal bravery medal, the PDSA Dickin Medal, since 1943. They include 32 pigeons, 18 dogs, 3 horses, and 1 cat, all with their own amazing tales that are definitely worth searching for. Other creatures celebrated here include dolphins, elephants, and even glowworms, once used by World War I troops to read their letters in the dark.

IT'S REALLY ME!

JEREMY BENTHAM, UNIVERSITY COLLEGE LONDON

It's not often you can meet a historical figure in the flesh or, in this case, the bones. The philosopher Jeremy Bentham asked for his skeleton to be preserved, and when he died in 1832, he got his wish. His skeleton sits here in a cabinet, dressed in his old clothes. For years before he died, Bentham carried around glass eyes in his pocket, to be used in his skull when the time came to display it. Unfortunately, the dead head ended up looking too scary, so the friendly head on the skeleton is made of wax.

UNIVERSITY COLLEGE LONDON

BLUE BOYS AND GIRLS

ALDGATE AND SEVERAL OTHER LOCATIONS

A number of blue-coated children are set up in nooks and crannies around town. They mark the location of charity schools, mostly set up in the 1700s. Poor children were educated here and they wore blue coats as a uniform, probably because blue dye was cheap at the time. They wore bright yellow socks, too, so they would have been easy to spot!

search: CHARITY SCHOOLS

LONDON'S FIRST

The very first charity school was founded in 1552 by Edward VI on Newgate Street, London. Charity schools soon spread throughout the urban areas of England and Wales.

WHICH ONE ARE YOU?

THE BROAD FAMILY, BROADGATE ESTATE

This set of statues represents us! It's a modern family, as imagined by Spanish sculptor Xavier Corbero. One of the blocks is a dog and one has children's shoes carved at its base. It's the stone version of everyone who lives in or visits the fabulous capital of London!

HERO TO ZERO

SIR WALTER RALEIGH, GREENWICH

Sir Walter Raleigh was one of Britain's original explorers. He was a naval hero who sailed to North America in 1578 and helped establish the first European settlements there. He is best known for introducing Queen Elizabeth I to tobacco and potatoes, brought over from America. The story goes that Raleigh's servant drenched him with a bucket of beer when he first saw his master smoking, thinking he was on fire. Serves Raleigh right for his filthy habit! His luck ran out when Elizabeth I's successor, James I, had him executed for treason.

INDEX

INDEX